LOST
TRIBES &
SUNKEN
CONTINENTS

LOST TRIBES & SUNKEN CONTINENTS

MYTH AND METHOD
IN THE STUDY OF AMERICAN INDIANS

Robert Wauchope

THE UNIVERSITY OF CHICAGO PRESS

CHICAGO & LONDON

International Standard Book Number: 0-226-87635-7 (clothbound)
Library of Congress Catalog Card Number: 62-18112

The University of Chicago Press, Chicago 60637
The University of Chicago Press, Ltd., London

TO MY MOTHER

ELIZABETH BOSTEDO WAUCHOPE

CONTENTS

1 INTRODUCTION: BATTLEGROUND OF THE THEORISTS   1

2 ELEPHANTS AND ETHNOLOGISTS: EGYPT IN AMERICA   7

3 LOST CONTINENTS: ATLANTIS AND MU   28

4 LOST TRIBES AND THE MORMONS   50

5 DR. PHUDDY DUDDY AND THE CRACKPOTS   69

6 MEN OUT OF ASIA   83

7 KON-TIKI AND THE LINGUISTIC ACROBATS   103

8 THE RIGHTEOUS AND THE RACISTS   115

9 THE MYSTICS: CONCLUSION   125

REFERENCES   139

INDEX   147

ILLUSTRATIONS

Queen Moo at the execution of Prince Coh   12

Chac Mool   17

Maya and Egyptian pyramids   22

Augustus Le Plongeon   22

Le Plongeons' headquarters in Maya ruins   22

Alice Le Plongeon   23

Stone monument from Copan, Honduras   23

Maya depictions of the macaw   24

Quetzalcoatl holding up the sea   32

Map of Atlantis   34

Map of the Lost Continents   37

The "Hieratic Alphabet" of Mu   40

Map of Mu   43

Brasseur de Bourbourg 45

The Jaredite Era 58

The Nephite Era 60

Stylized bas-relief tree, Temple of the Cross, Palenque, Mexico 65

Flood myth from ancient Maya book, the Codex Dresden 70

Southeastern Mexican stone disk showing bearded Semitic-like profile 70

Quetzalcoatl from the Codex Magliabecchiano 70

Stylized trees in the Mexican Codex Fejéváry 71

Mexican Morning Star Sacrifice depicted in ancient Mexican Codex Nuttal 71

Dr. Phuddy Duddy and his captive audience 72

Diving gods, from Bali and Mexico 94

Lotus panel with human figures, from Chichen Itza 118

Figures showing similar scepters and sitting positions, from India and Mexico 118

Figures on tiger thrones, from India and Mexico 119

Water lily motif, from India and Yucatan 119

1

INTRODUCTION: BATTLEGROUND OF THE THEORISTS

WHEN COLUMBUS DISCOVERED the natives of the New World in 1492, there was no doubt in his mind that they were east Asiatics, and he promptly began referring to them as Indians. He is said to have carried this belief with him to his grave. But long before Columbus died, a number of Europeans suspected that the new lands were not Cathay at all, a suspicion strongly reinforced when Balboa reached the Pacific shore in 1513 and confirmed beyond doubt by Magellan's voyage six years later.

The realization that another vast sea lay beyond the western limits of America led at once to speculations regarding the origin of the American Indian. Was he a native of this new continent, and had he always been? If not, where did he come from, and how? Thus began a great debate that has endured for over four centuries, and one that has involved not only scholars but organizations, nations, and even religions. For the origin of the American Indian, which along with ancient

Egypt, Stonehenge, and the Easter Island monuments has always fascinated the mystics, is a subject highly charged with emotion, as are so many where science and religion, or amateur and professional, clash, and where racist, nationalistic, and ethnic values become involved. Although it is a body of theory much older than that of biological evolution, it has run a curiously similar course, with scientists often taking one broad position opposed to most lay and almost all religious hypotheses, yet finding no exact agreement among themselves, while the laymen, united in characterizing all professional scholars as either atheists or chuckleheads or both, are in turn accused of running off in all theoretical directions at once.

Just as the evolutionary controversy attracted such unexpected opponents as Clarence Darrow and William Jennings Bryan, the American Indian debates have pitted against each other priests and professors, physicians and lawyers, businessmen and artists, even a president and a vice-president of the United States. The most dignified professors who have allowed themselves to become embroiled seem to adapt rapidly to the biting sarcasm and uninhibited idiom that enliven what might otherwise be a fairly dull field of investigation. For example, Professor Ralph Linton, late distinguished anthropologist of Yale, in a book review published in *American Antiquity*, the official journal of American archeology, said of Harold S. Gladwin, who had written a book suggesting, among other things, that survivors of Alexander the Great's wrecked fleet found their way to America in the fourth century B.C. and were responsible for some of the great prehistoric civilizations of this hemisphere: "Mr. Gladwin approaches the problem of American origins with the tentative jocularity of an elderly gentleman patting a new secretary's posterior. If she objects, he can lament her lack of a sense of humor; if she does not, the next moves are obvious."

Besides the individuals who have championed the various Indian origin theories, some famous institutions and organizations are more than casually interested—for example the

Rosicrucians, the Theosophists, the Church of Jesus Christ of Latter-day Saints (the Mormons), and of course the anthropological profession itself. In addition to the institutional positions are many others which have been urged in eloquent prose in hundreds of books over the last four centuries, or read solemnly before congresses of learned societies here and in Europe, by scholars who were sure that our redskins were once Tyrian Phoenicians, Assyrians, ancient Egyptians, Canaanites, Israelites, Trojans, Romans, Etruscans, Greeks, Scythians, Tartars, Chinese Buddhists, Hindus, Mandingoes or other Africans, Madagascans, the early Irish, Welsh, Norsemen, Basques, Portuguese, French, Spaniards, Huns, or survivors of the Lost Continents of Mu or Atlantis, the last a uniquely difficult theory to debate, since their alleged great civilizations conveniently sank beneath the ocean some eleven thousand or more years ago, with Plato possibly the earliest authority we have for their existence. A few have taken the position that our Indians are descended from none of these, but instead that Man originated in the Americas, and the Old World is then actually the New.

The popularity cycle of these multifarious schemes suggests that they have at least something of the nature of fads. The earliest explorers and historians of America tended to favor the Lost Tribes of Israel hypothesis, for in those days ancient Hebrew ethnology as described in the Old Testament was about the only well-documented "primitive" way of life known and therefore the first to occur to a seeker of Indian relationships. Eighteenth- and early nineteenth-century classicists tended, on the other hand, to see Carthaginian-Phoenician traits in the art, architecture, language, religion, and political structure of the Central American Maya, the Aztec and pre-Aztec civilizations of Mexico, and the Inca and other high cultures of the South American Andes. With spectacular archeological discoveries in Egypt, there came a rash of writers convinced that all civilization stemmed from the Nile Valley and that our

American prehistoric ruins are merely remnants of Egyptian colonists.

Lost Atlantis has been a continuing favorite for generations, stimulated anew every few years by editions of the Spence and Donnelly best sellers; and the Israelite theory, too, commands a large and consistent following since it is a matter of Mormon church doctrine that our aborigines are descendants of the Hebrews and that their wanderings over Asia and the Americas are faithfully described in the divinely dictated *Book of Mormon*. The latest craze, the notion that American Indians sailed westward across the Pacific and populated the Polynesian islands, has a tremendous current following thanks to Thor Heyerdahl's great adventure narrative of his daring voyage on the balsa raft, *Kon-Tiki*. Some of the same museum visitors who used to corner uncomfortable scientists twenty years ago and berate them for their lack of faith in drowned Atlantis, now shake the same scolding fingers at those who do not express enthusiasm over *Aku-Aku*.

Strangely enough, the many and varied explanations of American Indian origins have not competed with one another too militantly. Supporters of the Carthaginian theory have also approved an Israelite movement to America (to account for the wilder tribes, however); some of the Egyptianists are quite willing to recognize also Lost Atlantis; the Rosicrucians and Theosophists have a lot to say about both Atlantis and its Pacific counterpart, Mu. But in stark contrast to this permissive tolerance of other theories in general, the lay writers on these subjects have one great bias in common: they all scorn, ridicule, and complain bitterly about the professional anthropologists of American museums and universities, whom they regard variously as stupid, stubborn, hopelessly conservative, and very frequently plain dishonest.

This puzzles the professionals, who find nothing particularly offensive about their concept of an Asiatic cradle for the American Indian, much as Thomas Jefferson outlined in his *Note on the State of Virginia*, with the peopling of America taking place in a series of invasion waves via Bering Strait and

Alaska over the twenty-five to fifty thousand or so years since the middle and closing stages of the Ice Age. A growing number of anthropologists also think that certain American high civilizations, like the Maya, received some additional stimulus from trans-Pacific contacts with southeast Asia. To the mystics this is an intolerably conservative and unimaginative theoretical position.

These are the warring theories and this is their battleground. The fighting has been fierce, the casualties heavy. The famed nineteenth-century scholar, Abbé Brasseur de Bourbourg, lost his friends and his reputation. The English nobleman, Edward King, Viscount Kingsborough, about whom we shall read in a later chapter, spent a fortune on his obsession with the Lost Tribes of Israel theory and died, some say of a broken heart, in a Dublin debtor's prison. The French adventurer, sometime doctor of medicine, engineer, lawyer, and archeologist, Augustus Le Plongeon and his worshipping young wife, Alice, after spending many years in the thorny thickets of the dry Yucatan peninsula, exploring the ancient ruins of the forgotten Maya past, lived their last years disappointed and deeply embittered over the rejection of their wild theories about American civilization moving to Egypt many thousands of years ago. James Adair devoted forty years of his life to firsthand study of the American Indians, but his claims that they were the Lost Tribes of Israel brought him ridicule and even accusations of dishonesty. Stung by scientific criticism, Thor Heyerdahl braved the Pacific on a balsa raft to support his theories that the South American Indians peopled the Pacific, and today several devout Mormon scholars stand, like some of their ill-fated predecessors, against the world of science and learning in their belief that *The Book of Mormon* is the true history of Israelite peoples in America.

An ever increasing number of people in this country and abroad are intrigued, in some cases compulsively obsessed, with all forms of symbolism, especially if it is somehow esoteric, and best of all if it can be related to the culture and origins of the American Indian, particularly the Maya, Aztec, and Inca, to whose colorful prehistoric civilizations they are drawn like flies to honey. Here they can delve spellbound in bizarre symbols, the most dramatic and sacred rituals, mysterious hieroglyphs, jungle-shrouded ancient temples, non—Indo-European languages whose strange syllables lend themselves to endless games of linguistic blind-man's buff, and polytheistic religions with strong mathematical, astrological, sadistic, and phallic overtones. Their fascination with these becomes an addiction, in some cases literally a religion, and in holding fast to their beliefs about aboriginal America, in the face of often brusque rebuffs from professional anthropologists, they feel persecuted, martyred to a sort of semi-scientific, semi-religious destiny that must not be denied. Their writings are frequently larded with references to the Almighty, theology, and ethics in passages where the uninitiated reader fails to see the relevance. Dealers in used books are well aware of them, for they haunt the sections in bookshops marked "Esoteric, Occult, and Curiosa."

Some of these men have been out-and-out charlatans, opportunists interested less in the quest for truth than in the money and notoriety their writings and lectures brought them. Others have been stupid, unable to distinguish fact from fantasy. Still others were conscientious scholars, indefatigable workers, and men of great integrity, but victims of the ignorance of their time, often further handicapped by years of isolation from the scholarly world as they explored the vast jungles and remote highland Indian villages in their search for knowledge of the American past. Most of them—charlatan, clod, and scholar alike—have shared certain attitudes and personality traits that give them, as a group, a certain identity.

One wonders what theories are these that so capture imagination and fierce allegiance, and what sort of men are so obsessed with mystic and religious interpretations of the ancient American past that they will follow them, sometimes literally, to the death against all opposition. In the pages that follow we shall take a closer look at both the theories and the people who have so steadfastly championed them.

2

ELEPHANTS AND
ETHNOLOGISTS:
EGYPT IN AMERICA

PERHAPS THE MOST popular theory about
American Indian origins derives the famous ancient civilizations of Mexico, Central America, and the Andes from Egypt.
There were pyramids in both America and Egypt, there were
mummies in Peru and Egypt, sun worship was practiced in
many parts of the New World as well as in Egypt, and both
areas produced hieroglyphic writing, royal tombs, bas-relief
sculpture, and a number of other similar customs and cultural
traits. To most people the word "archeology" conjures up but
one picture: towering pyramids, the brooding Sphinx, King
Tut's tomb, and the Valley of the Nile. It is only natural that
when they see ancient relics like these somewhere else, even
in faraway America, they see a connection with the classic
expression of ancient civilizations—Dynastic Egypt.

Of the numerous Egyptian enthusiasts, one of the most devoted, the most fiercely loyal, and the most militant was a
French adventurer, Augustus Le Plongeon, whose bitter de-

nunciations of his foes and whose arrogant flaunting of his own ego produced a lurid epoch in the history of American archeology. Let us meet this vivid character through a typical incident that he himself describes.

The stories differ, but Augustus Le Plongeon's own version is that he had just excavated the statue of an ancient Maya god from the tumbled debris of Chichen Itza's great stone ruins in the scorched thickets of northern Yucatan, and his superstitious Indian laborers refused to touch it, much less lift it out of the hallowed earth and marl that had concealed it for over six hundred years. It was a great archeological treasure, and the long-bearded Frenchman, his face and balding head almost black from his many years of exploration on the sun-baked tropic peninsula, was determined not to be cheated of his discovery.

Le Plongeon did not know then that Fate had already decreed he was not to have this huge reclining stone god after all; his immediate problem was to persuade the natives to do his bidding and get it out of the ground. Looking more like Moses after forty years in the wilderness than a fifty-year-old adventurer and mystic with a young and lovely bride, the self-styled doctor was a stubborn man, perhaps one of the most obstinate and ornery individuals who ever lived; he was also one of the most imaginative. A more prosaic person might have tried to persuade the Indians and reason with them, but this approach was completely foreign to Le Plongeon's unique and volatile personality. Stroking his long, gray beard and regarding his rebellious workers balefully, he suddenly had an idea. People obey gods: I shall convince them that I am a reincarnated Maya god! Imperiously he motioned them to follow him.

The little group clambered over the piles of whitened limestone ruins, through the tangled underbrush and thorny scrub thickets, and labored to the summit of a crumbling structure overlooking the drab olive-green plain of Yucatan. A sculptured stone panel stood exposed in the ancient wreckage. Let

Le Plongeon tell the story himself, as he recorded it in a book published in 1878:

In order to overcome their scruples, and also to prove if my suspicions were correct, that as their forefathers and the Egyptians of old, they still believed in reincarnation, I caused them to accompany me to the summit of the great pyramid. . . . On one of the antae, at the entrance on the north side, is the portrait of a warrior wearing a long, straight, pointed beard. The face, like that of all the personages represented, is in profile. I placed my head against the stone so as to present the same position of my face . . . and called the attention of my Indians to the similarity of his and my own features. They followed every lineament of the faces with their fingers to the very point of the beard, and soon uttered an exclamation of astonishment: "Thou, here," and slowly scanned again the features sculptured on the stone and my own. "So, so," they said, "thou too art one of our great men, who has been disenchanted. Thou, too, were a companion of the great Lord Chaacmol. That is why thou didst know where he was hidden and thou hast come to disenchant him also. His time to live again on earth has then arrived." From that moment on every word of mine was implicitly obeyed.

Next day another group of Indians arrived to see the great man. He again took them to the bas-relief and went through his pose of the day before. The strangers "fell on their knees before me, and, in turn, kissed my hand."

One gets the impression from the doctor's writings that he was happiest in the field, where among humble and ignorant native laborers he found the real or fantasied adulation that he craved so vainly in the United States. Anecdotes that he tells on himself reveal an astonishing egotism amounting almost to delusions of grandeur. It would almost be kinder to Le Plongeon to regard this whole story as a fabrication, for I cannot think of any more comical and at the same time more pitiful scene than this, of confused and doubtless embarrassed Indians murmuring probably incomprehensible words while the

Gallic Don Quixote struck heroic poses beside a stone god of the ancient Maya.

I am undecided whether Le Plongeon concocted these anecdotes from wishful fantasy or whether, as seems likely, he was so inept with spoken Maya that he simply misunderstood much of what the Indians said. There is considerable evidence favoring each of these possibilities. For one thing the stories evidently varied in the telling. A friend of Le Plongeon heard the above incident quite differently: that the Indians noticed the resemblance between Le Plongeon and the sculptured figure, and that all the Frenchman's disclaimers could not persuade the natives that he was not the reincarnated Maya. For another thing, the stories are inconsistent with what we know about the Maya at this period, and by now information about them from less fanciful travelers was abundant. In 1876 they were all Roman Catholics and had been exposed to Catholic instruction and supervision for over three centuries. They surely entertained no notions of reincarnation, which is and apparently always has been a concept foreign to their religious ideology, the story of Cortez being considered the reincarnated Quetzalcoatl to the contrary notwithstanding. Moreover, by 1880 probably no Yucatec Indian was superstitious about the Maya ruins and antiquities around him, in contrast to the highland Maya farther south in Guatemala, who even today are disturbed by desecrations of their ancient places of worship.

Indian laborers in Yucatan are very anxious to please their superiors in government or their employers in work; they try desperately to understand what is being said to them in poor Spanish (which they themselves often do not understand too well) or in worse Yucatec Maya. Perhaps because of the language barriers, they quickly learn to watch their employer's gestures and expressions and try to divine what he wants them to do or say. Anyone, with or without a long, pointed beard, going through the motions that Le Plongeon described, would doubtless get approximately the same co-operative response from Indian workmen hoping to please the boss. The words and expressions Le Plongeon has them say were surely either put in their mouths by him, through an interpreter, or were completely misunderstood. Even their talk, as quoted by the doctor, is misleading; if they spoke in the second person to him, this was not out of formality or solemnity (as it sounds in English) but because that is the only construction they use. The respectful third person pronoun is rarely heard among them even today.

Whatever one may think of these tactics, or of the obvious satisfaction that the near-paranoiac Frenchman derived from his real or fancied adoration by these ignorant natives, the maneuver was apparently effective, and the stone god emerged from its pit—to be fought over again by Le Plongeon and the Mexican government officials who refused to let him take it from the country. This reclining statue was one of a series of similar figures that have since been discovered both in Yucatan and in Mexico proper, called Chac Mool figures, and though their identity is debated by experts today, Le Plongeon had no doubt that they represented an Indian prince-god who figured prominently in both ancient Egyptian and prehistoric Maya-Toltec history and religion. For Le Plongeon believed in a direct historical connection between the civilizations of Mexico, Central America, and Egypt. He maintained further that the shape of Maya temples was deliberately laid out to represent the Egyptian letter M, which, he said, was called "ma" and meant "place, country, and by extension, the Universe." He was sure that the ancient sacred mysteries, the origin of Free Masonry consequently, originated in America and were carried by Maya colonists to the Nile, the Euphrates, and the shores of the Indian Ocean not less than 11,500 years ago.

Le Plongeon reconstructed in detail a blood-and-thunder rendition of Maya history based solely on sculptures, murals, and hieroglyphic texts that authorities on Maya epigraphy today do not pretend to be able to read. It is a lengthy story and its romantic impact suffers in synopsis: The king of Chichen Itza and Uxmal, now two Maya ruins in Yucatan, had three sons, Cay, Aac, and Coh, and two daughters, Moo and Nicte. By Maya law, the youngest son should marry the eldest daughter to insure legitimate and divine descent of the royal family, a practice also known among the Egyptians and Peruvians. Prince Coh thus married Moo, but Aac, who also loved her, murdered him. (Le Plongeon excavated a stone projectile point and an urn with what appeared to be ashes in it; he claimed at once that these were Coh's cremated heart and the spearhead with which he was slain.) In the civil war that followed, Aac, now king of Uxmal, courted Queen Moo of Chichen Itza, but

Le Plongeon's drawing of a Maya temple decoration which he thought depicted Prince Coh's execution by his rival brother, Aac. The widow, Queen Moo, and attendants are mourners.

she spurned him. A Maya sculpture which Le Plongeon asserted was a depiction of this scene, could as well, he added, represent Adam and Eve in the Garden of Eden; indeed, according to Le Plongeon the Old Testament story is the same anecdote, but distorted by some misanthrope old bachelor, possibly the author of Genesis, who changed the Maya version out of spite for having been jilted himself by some lady love.

Fleeing from her brother's wrath, Moo hoped to find shelter in the east, in some remnant of the Lost Continent of Atlantis (Le Plongeon subscribed to that, too), but failing this she continued traveling and at last reached the Maya colonies that for many years had been established on the banks of the Nile.

Here the settlers received her with open arms, called her "little sister" (Isis), and proclaimed her their queen. Eventually, though, she fell into Aac's hands, he abused her and put her to death along with Cay, his elder brother.

Le Plongeon blandly states in his preface to *Queen Moo and the Egyptian Sphinx:* "In this work I offer no theory. In questions of history theories prove nothing. They are therefore out of place. I leave my readers to draw their own inferences from the facts presented for their consideration." Then typically, "Whatever be their conclusions is no concern of mine. . . ."

Actually, in spite of his frequent defiant utterances of this kind, his readers' opinions were of vital concern to Le Plongeon. He bristled at the slightest exception anyone took to his beliefs, he wrote long letters complaining that he was being persecuted by scholars and officials alike, and forty years after his death his close friends remembered that his last years were embittered by his failure to win scientific recognition.

A contemporary of Le Plongeon, John T. Short, in his widely read book, *The North Americans of Antiquity,* expressed regret that the self-styled doctor's enthusiasm was so apparent in his reports, adding, "a judicial frame of mind, as well as the calmness which accompanies it, are requisite both for scientific work and the inspiration of confidence in the reader." This infuriated the Frenchman, who responded with this outburst:

Thanks for the advice! But I will ask Mr. Short what in fact does he know about Yucatan, and the history of its primitive inhabitants? Is there anywhere a man, who, today, knows about these things so as to pretend to pass an opinion on them? What does Mr. Short know of the monuments of Yucatan. Has he ever read a true description? Where? It has never been published to my knowledge. Who is to know best about them, Mr. Short, who has never seen them, or Dr. Le Plongeon, who has made a special study of them, *in situ* during seven years?

Actually, by 1881, when this was written, the literature on Yucatecan antiquities was extensive and in some cases quite competent. John Short and Augustus Le Plongeon both could very easily have read, for example, the enormously popular four volumes of *Incidents of Travel* (1841, 1843) by John Lloyd Stephens and the remarkably accurate engravings of Maya ruins by his architect companion, Frederick Catherwood.

Who was this highly imaginative, fire-breathing dragon, so cantankerously defying his enemies, both real and imagined? Strangely enough, of this eloquently voluble and widely traveled mystic, who became embroiled in so many verbal and legal battles and who wrote voluminous letters to any who would read them, we know very little of his pre-archeological career. Born on the island of Jersey in 1826—his maternal great-uncle was Lord Jersey—and having attended military college at Caen and the Polytechnic Institute of Paris, he and a fellow student acquired a yacht, which they sailed to the west coast of South America. Off the coast of Chile a violent storm arose. For many tortuous hours they battled the fierce winds and heavy seas, vainly seeking a haven along that treacherous shore. Finally in a sustained roar of near-hurricane intensity, the monstrous waves engulfed the small vessel and as she foundered, it was every man for himself. Whatever can be said of Le Plongeon's passionate mind, his colossal conceit, and his perverse obstinacy, one must grant him also a tremendous courage. He pitted his own strength, which must have been great indeed to carry him through so many years in the fever-ridden tropics, against the raging sea, and he won. Of that entire company only Le Plongeon and his co-captain survived; the Frenchman staggered ashore battered, exhausted, half-drowned, but still very much alive and, within a short time, his old confident, egotistical self.

It is typical of Le Plongeon's stubborn will that instead of returning dejected to France and home, he saw in this new land a test of his wits and his initiative. He obtained a job teaching drawing, mathematics, and language at a college in Valparaiso, and it comes as no surprise to anyone who studies the single-minded intensity of the man to learn that when he

started out again, it was not as a timid traveler who had for-
sworn sailing the seas again forever, as many a person might
under similar circumstances, but again as a skipper, in com-
mand of a vessel bound for California. Nor does it arouse too
much wonder in those who have followed his subsequent violent career to read that this second voyage also encountered
formidable storms; as his widow recorded later, "the ship was
reduced to a pitiable condition." This was still the era of great
risk on the high seas. Frederick Catherwood, the gifted English
architect who immortalized himself and focused worldwide interest on the Maya ruins of Yucatan and Central America with
his masterly lithographs of the ancient cities visited by him
and his companion, John Lloyd Stephens of New York, was
lost at sea in a similar voyage when the SS "Arctic" sank off
Newfoundland in 1854. But this time Le Plongeon and his ship
made port together.

San Francisco was another challenge to Augustus Le
Plongeon. Apparently well schooled in drawing and mathematics, he eventually became City and County Surveyor. He
made a valuable acquaintance in Stephen J. Field, afterward
a Justice of the United States Supreme Court. But he could
not settle down, and he returned to Europe and England. Again
the urge to move seized him, and he sailed to the island of
Saint Thomas, then to Veracruz, and later crossed Mexico to
Acapulco on horseback. "Upon his return to San Francisco,"
his wife, Alice, wrote matter-of-factly in a necrology, "Dr. Le
Plongeon took up the practice of law and was successful; but
certain occurrences attracted him to the practice of medicine,
in which he quickly made a name for the remarkable manner
in which he restored various patients who had been pronounced
incurable." Since Mme Le Plongeon, in her fairly detailed account of her husband's earlier schooling, mentions no particular law school or medical college, it seems fair to infer that
Augustus Le Plongeon actually had very little formal training
in either law or medicine and may have conferred the degrees
M.D. and LL.D. on himself. In his writings he invariably re-

ferred to himself as Dr. Le Plongeon. When he was later commissioned to study archeology in Peru, he established there a private hospital, where, according to his widow, "he introduced the application of electricity in medicinal baths, and effected notable cures." In Yucatan he is said to have endeared himself to the natives by treating them for yellow fever, having survived a bout with it himself and considering himself at least partially immune to the dread disease.

In Peru Le Plongeon also became interested in earthquakes, invented a seismograph and seismometer by which, his wife tells us, he could foretell the approach and direction of an earthquake, and published articles on this subject in *Van Nostrand's Magazine*, New York. After more travel in New York, London, and Paris, he returned in 1875 to Yucatan, "at the peril of his life," Alice Le Plongeon wrote, "for the war of the races was very active at that time." For over thirty years more he explored the ruined Maya cities of the peninsula, published his spectacular theories, and waged a verbal war with American anthropologists and Mexican government officials, the latter of whom he accused of illegally confiscating the antiquities he excavated.

Le Plongeon went overboard seemingly for every notion that occurred to him or to anyone else. He was utterly incapable of critically examining either the factual or the logical evidence bearing on any theory he wanted to believe. When he found a line across a sculptured lintel in an ancient ruin in Yucatan and noticed some zigzag motifs near it, he immediately decided that the prehistoric Maya communicated by means of electric telegraph wires! More of the nature of Le Plongeon's reasoning is reflected in his analysis of the Chac Mool stone god he had so much trouble excavating:

As to the conventional posture given to all the statues of the rulers and other illustrious personages in Mayach [reclining on the back, with the knees drawn up, and face turned to one side] it confirms the fact of their geographical attainments. If we compare, for instance, the outlines of the effigy of Prince Coh discovered by the author at Chichen-Itza in 1875, with the contour of the eastern coasts of the American continent, placing the head at Newfoundland, the knees at Cape St. Roque, and the feet at Cape Horn, it is easy to perceive that they are identical. The shallow basin held on the belly of the statue, between the hands, would then be symbolical of the Gulf of Mexico and of the Caribbean Sea.

Chac Mool, the reclining statue of an ancient Maya-Mexican god, discovered by the imaginative Augustus Le Plongeon, who believed that the Maya came from Lost Atlantis and later created Egyptian civilization. He declared that the outline of this sculpture represented the North and South American continents, separated by the Gulf of Mexico, and thus revealed the Maya's profound knowledge of geography. *After Proskouriakoff.*

A letter to the Honorable John W. Foster, Minister of the United States at Mexico, dated May 1, 1877, at the Island of Cozumel—today a fast-growing tourist resort off the east coast of Yucatan—shows Le Plongeon's mind churning with questions, speculations, and notions of every kind. In the middle of an epistle that must have been thirty handwritten pages long, doubtless composed by candlelight or torch, we find the following passages:

These inner edifices belong to a very ancient period, and among the débris I have found the head of a bear exquisitely sculptured out of a block of marble. It is in an unfinished state. When did bears inhabit the peninsula? Strange to say, the Maya does not furnish the name for the bear. Yet one-third of this tongue is pure Greek. Who brought the dialect of Homer to America? Or who took to Greece that of the Mayas? Greek is the offspring of Sanscrit. Is Maya? or are they coeval? A clue for ethnologists to follow the migrations of the human family on this old continent. Did the bearded men whose portraits are carved on the massive pillars of the fortress of Chichen-Itza belong to the Mayan Nations? The Maya language is not devoid of words from the Assyrian. . . .

The customs, religion, architecture of this country have nothing in common with those of Greece. Who carried the Maya to the country of Helen? Was it the Caras or Carians, who have left traces of their existence in many countries of America? They are the most ancient navigators known. They roved the seas long before the Phoenicians. They landed on the North-East coasts of Africa, thence they entered the Mediterranean, where they became dreaded as pirates, and afterwards established themselves on the shores of Asia Minor. Whence came they: What was their origin? Nobody knows. They spoke a language unknown to the Greeks, who laughed at the way they pronounced their own idiom. Were they emigrants from this Western continent? Was not the tunic of white linen, that required no fastening, used by the Ionian women, according to Herodotus, the same as the *uipil* of the Maya females of to-day even, introduced among the inhabitants of some of the Mediterranean isles?

These words pouring from his pen on that faraway tropical island show how uncritically Le Plongeon accepted any similarity as evidence of historical contact, how he assumed unquestioningly that his own identifications (of the bear, for example) were correct (which it was not), and how, instead of questioning his own theories when he confronted a mass of contrary evidence, he merely admitted bewilderment and walked calmly away from the subject, still convinced of his original hypothesis.

Although he foresaw with ample reason the opposition that his writings would meet, or, worse, that they would simply be ignored, Augustus Le Plongeon rushed to meet his unseen foes with anticipated counterthreats.

If the perusal of this book fails to awaken in this country an interest in ancient American civilization and history, then I will follow the advice said to have been given by Jesus of Nazareth to his disciples when sending them on their mission of spreading the gospel among the nations: "And whomsoever [sic] shall not receive you, nor hear you, when ye do part hence, shake off the dust under your feet. . . " St. Mark, chap. vi, verse 11—for I shall consider it useless to spend more time, labor, and money on the subject in the United States, remembering the fate of Professor Morse, when he asked Congress for permission to introduce his electric telegraph in this country.

In 1881, speaking before the American Antiquarian Society in Worcester, he said, ". . . since I felt that I was abandoned by ALL, notwithstanding ALL wanted to procure from me GRATIS what had cost me so much time, labor and money to acquire, I made up my mind to keep my knowledge, so dearly purchased, to destroy some day or other my collections, and to let those who wish to know more about the ancient cities of Yucatan, do what I have done. . . ." As a matter of fact, Le Plongeon actually did something of this sort in retaliation against Mexican officials who had confiscated the monuments, statues, and other relics that he found in Yucatan. After his death in 1908, his widow revealed: "Another great statue which he found and hid again, is yet concealed, its whereabouts being known only to the present writer."

On her deathbed, Alice Le Plongeon turned over to an intimate friend many of her husband's drawings and notes and evidently tried to tell the location of another spectacular discovery they claimed to have made and covered again in 1875— some underground rooms containing stone boxes holding perfectly preserved ancient records of the Maya. As "she spoke with agonizing difficulty . . . I jotted down each word as I heard it clearly; in my hand was only an envelope," this friend later wrote. However, the records which Mme Le Plongeon gave to her friend, if indeed they do contain any clues to the reburied antiquities, were so disguised and complicated as to be useless today. As the friend explained, when she made the notes available a great many years later, "Le Plongeon believed in making people puzzle out things . . . and he had rather odd ideas for protecting the secrets."

Mme Le Plongeon wrote in a necrology of her husband that his sympathetic and benevolent disposition made him universally beloved. This view, however, was not shared by one of Le Plongeon's most enthusiastic admirers, who wrote, twenty-three years after his death: "I rather think that the Doctor's stormy temper often antagonized men who would (and could) have been won by patience to some of his views." This friend described Le Plongeon's "loyal little wife" as only seventeen when she married the doctor, thirty years older than she. "Mme Le Plongeon was a good deal of a mystic" herself, he wrote, and "there was a great deal of tragedy in her life." They both felt stung by the world's indifference to their work. "The Le Plongeons told me with much bitterness some of the things said to them, and of them!"

Most subsequent students of the Maya, professional and amateur alike, have turned thumbs down on Dr. Le Plongeon's proposals or, for the most part, have simply ignored them. The handwriting on Belshazzar's Chaldean banquet hall as reported in the Book of Daniel was of Maya derivation, as were Jesus' words on the cross: *Eli, eli lama sabachthani,* which did not mean, "My God, my God, why hast Thou forsaken me?"— words ill befitting the dying Christ in view of his courage, resignation, and faith—but instead were the Maya words, *Helo, helo, lamah xabac ta ni,* "Now, now, sinking, black ink over nose," that is to say, "Now I am sinking, darkness covers my face." That Le Plongeon did not consider these conclusions unreasonable is no better illustrated than in his desire not to have his name linked with that of the Abbé Brasseur de Bourbourg, whose ideas on the Lost Atlantis theory were, compared with Le Plongeon's, ultra-conservative. A little over forty years later Lewis Spence, the enormously popular proponent of the Lost Atlantis theory, voiced the same fear that he would be considered just another Brasseur, then he added Le Plongeon's name to that of the Abbé.

The Egyptian theories of American Indian connections range all the way from attributing American Indian civilization to Egypt, a point of view usually taken on snap judgment by the average visitor to museums in this country and championed in recent years by a distinguished Australian brain anatomist, G. Elliot Smith, to deriving Egyptian civilization from America, an idea best known through the writings of the eminent Abbé Charles Stephen Brasseur de Bourbourg in the 1860's. Writing fifty years apart, Brasseur and Smith nevertheless resembled each other in a number of ways, both being able, well-informed, tireless students, but both swept away into what most anthropologists nowadays consider untenable theories. Each became embroiled in a battle, the Abbé fighting his with himself, and Dr. Smith carrying on a bitter running combat throughout the latter part of his life with the established anthropological authorities in the United States.

Smith's proposal was that high civilization originated only once on the earth, and this happened to be in the Nile Valley. From here the seeds of Egyptian culture were spread throughout the world by the "Children of the Sun," adventurers seeking gold and pearls, first in the Old World and into the Pacific Islands, then on to the Americas, where Egyptian influences became manifest in pyramids, mummification,[1] gods and their attributes, and many religious and art motifs.

[1] Smith and Perry, maintaining that mummification was invented only once, in Egypt, traced its travels and particularly its route to the Americas by means of its occurrences in the Canary Islands and West Africa, India, southeastern Asia and Indonesia, Melanesia, Australia, and Polynesia. Smith studied the Egyptian embalming techniques, stressed their intricacy, and insisted that the reappearance of this "trait complex" along a chain of occurrences from Egypt to Peru, Mexico, eastern United States, and Alaska

Smith and his followers, notably William J. Perry, amassed a staggering body of evidence to support their hypothesis, but the American anthropologists hotly contested every item. The intellectual fortress for defending the independent development of indigenous American civilizations was the Peabody Museum of Archaeology and Ethnology at Harvard. There, in an austere and forbidding old red brick structure that looks today, from the outside, more like an ancient New England factory than one of the greatest museums in the world, had been developed the foremost anthropological center of research and teaching in the United States. Some famous older scholars at the university had surrounded themselves with vigorous new faculty and museum staff members, who were torn between traditional Harvard-Boston dignity and their indignation at the theories being perpetrated by some of their British colleagues.

Finally, Dr. Alfred Marston Tozzer, who was to become the dean of Mayanists, pointed out to his colleague, Dr. Roland B. Dixon, that Smith's books would soon have everyone in the world believing that the American Indians came straight from the Nile. Dixon reluctantly agreed to write a counter-statement and set to work assembling the data for what was eventually to become a book called *The Building of Cultures*.

Roland B. Dixon was a perfectionist and a meticulous scholar. A well-to-do bachelor, he was almost a stereotype of the college professor; he wore tweedy clothes, puffed on a pipe, moved slowly and spoke deliberately—an uninspiring, indeed a boring, lecturer, who gave his students every painfully minute detail of the subject matter and expected them to

---

could be explained only by historical content or diffusion. Among the features he emphasized were evisceration through a flank cut or by the perineum, throwing the viscera into the water, removal of the brain through an incision at the skull base, brine-soaking the body, rubbing it with oil, placing aromatic substances in the body cavity, painting the body red, inserting artificial eyes, incising in or between the toes, fingers, and at the elbows or knees for draining decomposition fluids, drying by heat, removing of the epidermis except at the tips of the fingers and toes.

(Courtesy Pan American World Airways)

According to the Egypt-in-America theorists, Maya pyramids like
El Castillo (*above*) of Chichen Itza, Yucatan, were derived from
those of the Nile Valley (*below*).

Augustus Le Plongeon (*upper left*), whose unusual theories and volatile personality embroiled him in a running battle with American anthropologists. His young wife, Alice (*above*), and their field headquarters in an ancient Maya ruin in Yucatan, about 1875 (*lower left*). In the back is a hammock with mosquito bar. Mme Le Plongeon, whose guitar is at the left with her husband's gun, recorded and composed music with Maya lyrics.

Upper part of a prehistoric stone monument at Copan, Honduras, carved (*at the top*) with figures which the Egyptianists claimed were elephants with mahouts perched on their heads, whereas Americanists insisted they were stylized macaws. One English scholar accused American archeologists of defacing this sculpture to destroy the damaging evidence. *After A. P. Maudslay.*

remember it all. But he was a profoundly well-informed anthropologist. It was something of a tradition among his graduate students, year after year, to try to catch him on a point of fact or in the identification of a curio from some exotic culture. Almost every day one could find him standing on the old stone steps of the museum between classes, surrounded by a little knot of his students who had handed him some unusual object —a bit of ornamented bronze, a fragment of carved ivory, a potsherd. Dixon would puff away at his pipe, turn the object over and over in his hands, stare at it deliberately and shake his head endlessly, as if he had never seen anything like it in all his life. Finally after perhaps minutes of this deliberation he would hand it back to the student dejectedly, and mutter, "Beats me. It's north Cambodian all right—Annam sixteenth century—but I can't imagine where they got those lotus designs." A little later a chagrined student would be paying off lost debts in draft beer down at Harvard Square.

Dixon set grimly to his task of demolishing the Smith-Perry contentions, and it was an enormous undertaking, for the Englishmen had made the most sweeping statements involving all sorts of evidence from all over the world. First he examined every known occurrence of mummification on earth, tracked down the individual customs connected with it in each case, and noted that a majority of the significant Egyptian details of the practices were generally absent, and that the actual methods employed were everywhere simple, "wholly natural, comparable to those used in preserving meat, and only what must have been done were any attempt made to keep the body." Thus he exploded a widespread popular belief that the ancients knew some secret of mummification unknown today, a process that would not have been practiced all over the world unless the Egyptians spread it themselves. The only significant analogy with Egyptian procedure was among a primitive folk on the islands of the Torres Straits, so far removed from all known lines of historical movement or cultural diffusion that they were almost untouched by drifting cultural influences from the west.

He found, too, inconsistencies in the age of the mummification traits and the alleged time of the Egyptian expansion. As for the hundreds of known stone structures that Smith asserted were related to the African pyramids, not a single Egyptian object, even so much as a bead, had been found in them. Dixon pointed out that Maya and Mexican pyramids are dated at least as early as the second and third centuries A.D., but

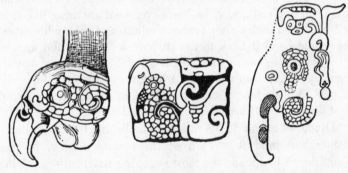

Progressive conventionalization of the macaw as depicted in Maya art. The Egyptian theorists declare that the third figure is an elephant. *After H. J. Spinden.*

those in Cambodia were not built until five or six hundred years later. The most ancient Dravidian temples of southern India, also cited as Egyptian-derived, were erected from the seventh century A.D. onward, nearly fifteen hundred years after Egyptian influence was stated by Smith to have reached India in complete form. He then administered the coup de grâce by showing that a local evolution of most pyramids can be traced through earlier prototypes in each region. For example, the massive stone graves or dolmens in China evolved from earlier passage graves and wooden prototypes instead of being introduced full blown from Egypt; besides, even Smith placed them in the ninth or even twelfth century B.C., but his Egyptian culture bearers were not supposed to have left Egypt until the ninth century or later.

The most celebrated point of difference between these schools of thought, in a battle that became truly vitriolic on both sides, with sarcasm dripping from each critique and book review and rejoinder, was whether some figures carved on a prehistoric monument at the Maya ruins of Copan in Honduras represented elephants with turbaned mahouts perched on their heads, as claimed by Smith, Perry, J. Leslie Mitchell, and others, or whether, as Professors Tozzer and Dixon of Harvard countered, they were actually stylized one-hundred-per-cent-American parrots. This last debate provided the title for one of Dr. Smith's books, *Elephants and Ethnologists*, in which he heaped unmerciful ridicule on the macaw-backers. Mitchell went so far as to suggest that American archeologists later deliberately mutilated this Maya stela to protect their precious theory, a charge that earned for him a reputation in scholarly circles roughly comparable to that which a Wimbledon tennis player would get if he set upon his opponent between games with a broken beer bottle.

The other side of the coin, the theory that civilization moved from the Western Hemisphere to the Nile, while it has practically no support nowadays, was vigorously argued by Brasseur de Bourbourg and later by Augustus Le Plongeon. Although working some twenty years earlier, the Abbé was by far the more erudite and the more conservative of the two. He believed firmly that the high civilizations of ancient Egypt and the Old World were derived from Atlantean colonists in America, and that certain Egyptian and Maya deities were actually the same beings manifested in separate cultures under different names.

Once you accept the premise that Egypt was colonized from America, or vice versa, more refined conclusions about when, where, and how this took place become routine chores. For example, Manuel Rejón Garciá of Mérida, Yucatan, writing in 1905, offered these calculations: Solomon ordered horses sold to Egypt one thousand years before Christ, but horses and pigs were not imported to Egypt before that. "From this it is easy to deduce that the populators of our part of America left Egypt before the importation there of the horse. Thus, America was peopled more than thirty centuries before the Christian era." Four years after Rejón, Channing Arnold and Frederick J. Tabor Frost, who claimed to be the first two Englishmen to write a book on Yucatan—they discounted Alfred Percival Maudslay's masterly photographic record made in 1899— asked whence came this American architecture, and then answered, paradoxically for a book entitled *The American Egypt:* "Egypt has been a great temptation to many, and in truth it is difficult, when you are first face to face with such very Egyptian-looking statues as the Atlantean figures which we found at Chichen . . . to resist the thought that there must be some connection between the stone marvels of the Nile Valley and the palaces of Yucatan. But putting aside the extraordinary difficulties in the way of mapping a possible route by which the connection between the two peoples could be effected, all available evidence is against you. The buildings of the two races are unlike in structure and design, in ornamentation and decoration; and if this dissimilarity could be explained away, and an attempt made to link the two ethnically, there is not a shred of evidence, physically, mythologically, philologically, or such as might be derived from a community of manners and customs, to help out the effort."

In spite of several generations of professional anthropological warfare against the theory of Egyptian influence in America, the notion stubbornly persists, chiefly because Egyptian archeology is the only field of prehistory with which most people have even a passing acquaintance. The resemblances between Maya and southeast Asiatic antiquities, for example, are far more numerous and more striking, but the public continues to insist that everything old in the Americas looks Egyptian. A lady in Mississippi once wrote that she had seen a fragment of plain white cloth said to have been in an Indian vessel excavated near her home, and she was sure it was Egyptian, for she had seen cloth just like it in the Egyptian section of the Metropolitan Museum. A recent issue of the *Smith Alumnae Quarterly* tells of an alumna's trip to Mexico. "They stopped," it says, "at lovely old Oaxaca and viewed the ancient ruins where Egyptian, Roman and Mayan-styled inscriptions are found together."

The theory of Egypt in America, or vice versa, like Atlantis and the Lost Tribes of Israel, is here to stay. For some reason difficult to fathom, people become emotionally attached to it and will not believe the most convincing arguments against it that professional scholars can provide. "A man convinced against his will is of the same opinion still."

3

LOST CONTINENTS: ATLANTIS AND MU

ALTHOUGH MOST PEOPLE who find a casual interest in the Maya and the ancient Peruvians look to Egypt for the inspiration of these American civilizations, the truly enthusiastic non-professionals are divided among a number of more specific theories, chief among them Lost Atlantis and the Lost Tribes of Israel. Both of these beliefs make use of Egyptian-American similarities but do not necessarily regard Egypt as the cradle of all higher cultures in the world.

By and large, the Lost Tribes and other Israelite hypotheses have appealed to a more conservative group of Old Testament-oriented antiquarians and amateur historians plus, of course, all the Mormons. Lost Atlantis devotees have been, for the most part, congenital romanticists and mystics. Nowadays they are to be found among adventure-readers and members of mystic organizations like the Rosicrucians and the Theosophists, but as late as the end of the nineteenth century they counted among their number a great many old-time scholars who flocked to the local meetings and international congresses of learned societies here and abroad to expound on an advanced civilization that flourished many thousands of years ago on a giant island in the Atlantic Ocean and that colonized the ancient American continent before being destroyed by cataclysmic volcanic eruptions, earthquakes, and tidal waves, to sink beneath the sea forever.

At the first International Congress of Americanists, for example, meeting at Nancy in 1875, there was a spirited discussion of the Chinese Fu-Sang theory—that the ancient Chinese had discovered a great land across the ocean, a story the frequent reappearance of which one delegate compared to the sea serpent apparition—then Dr. Chil y Narango of the Canary Islands brought up the question of Atlantis, already an aged and moot topic. Immediately emotions were stirred, scholarly tempers soared, and if we may judge from the considerably censored *Proceedings* printed long after the meetings adjourned and feelings had cooled, the congress was in an uproar.

This behavior was nothing new, nor did it end there. For fifty years more the Lost Continent controversy could be counted on to promote a verbal free-for-all; indeed it still could, except for the fact that professional anthropologists have simply tired of the battle, which promised to make the Hundred Years War look like a week-end skirmish. Today it is next to impossible to entice a professional into an argument on this topic; he will merely shrug and turn wearily away. For of all the American Indian origin theorists, advocates of the Lost Continent are by far the most devoted to their cause, and the most inflexible. Their loyalty in some cases attains a fierceness suggesting that the proponents of Atlantis or Mu have somehow come to think of themselves as citizens of those fabulous lands, dedicated to defend them to the death.

In the *Timaeus*, Plato has Egyptian priests of Sais converse with his ancestor, Solon, and tell him of a country larger than Asia Minor and Libya together, the seat of a magnificent civilization far out in the western sea. In his *Critias*, Plato tells more of this legendary continent, whose three kings were said to have ruled parts of Europe as far as the Baltic, Caspian, and Black seas, to have invaded Asia, and been defeated by Athenians, before they and some twelve millions of their subjects perished in the frightful calamity that befell their island home. Thus the most popular theory of them all finds American origins not on a continent or in a culture that can still be studied, even if only archeologically, but instead in a land that no longer exists save in the depths of the sea. Since primary sources are of course lacking (unless you accept as authentic certain "tablets" alleged to be original records of Mu) and secondary sources, if Plato can be considered one, are rare, the most fertile imaginations have had free rein in describing Atlantis, Mu, and their ancient wonders. These circumstances doubtless explain why of all the theories of Indian origins only the Lost Continents have attracted so much attention of artists, poets, and fiction writers.

Apparently there had been for many centuries tales of similar land masses beyond the Pillars of Hercules, stories of Arabian geographers, Greek tales of the Fortunate Islands, the Welsh Avalon, the Portuguese Isle of Seven Cities, and St. Brendan's Isle, but most especially a large land mass called Antilia, which appears on almost all maps of the fifteenth and early sixteenth centuries. Toscanelli's chart, which Christopher Columbus consulted in 1474, showed it in the direct track by sea from the Canary Islands to Japan, and Columbus is said to have shaped his course for the island and steered due west for about sixteen hundred miles looking for it.[1] Atlantis as the origin of New World culture is a theory dating back almost to the discovery of the New World itself. It was championed by Gonzalo Fernandez de Oviedo y Valdés in 1535, and by the

[1] A map of the world by Ruysch in 1508 still showed Antilia in this position; the chart bears a legend stating among other things that the island's population was ruled by an archbishop and six bishops, each with his own city, and that the people were strict Christians and "abounded in this world's wealth."

poet Giralamo Fracastoro five years earlier.[2] "Even in the 17th and 18th centuries," the *Encyclopaedia Britannica* notes wonderingly, "the credibility of the legend was seriously debated and sometimes admitted, even by Montaigne, Buffon, and Voltaire." The *Britannica*'s record is far out of date. Although the theory has been refuted by a host of scholars from Joseph de Acosta (1590) on, the definitive works favoring Atlantis, Lewis Spence's *Atlantis in America* and *The Problem of Atlantis*, were published respectively in New York and London in 1924 and 1925. In many ways Spence's claims are the least spectacular and his arguments the most reasoned in all the literature favoring this theory. He does not assert that Atlantis was the mother of all civilization, nor that Egypt was the fount of all culture. "The Atlantean hypothesis will gain nothing," he wrote, "by being pushed to extremes, or from the attentions of cranks. If it is worth examining at all, it is worth examining sanely." To get Atlantean culture to America Spence postulates another lost land mass, Antilia, of which the present Antilles are a remnant, and that served as the stepping stone to the western mainland. He believed that a Mexican Indian tradition of the destruction of the Toltec capital was probably reminiscent of the Atlantis calamity, or in some way confused with it.

There are more believers today in the Lost Continent than ever before, including the thousands of members of the Rosicrucian Order, whose revered late supreme executive or Imperator, H. Spencer Lewis, expressed the official belief that "a great continent called Atlantis . . . became submerged and brought to an end the earthly existence of millions of incarnated beings." Most or perhaps all members of the Theosophi-

---

[2] Also Francisco Lopez de Gómara (1553). J. Imbelloni's exhaustive book on Indian origin theories, *La Segunda Esfinge Indiana*, names the poet Giralamo Fracastoro (1530) and Agustin de Zarito (1555). According to the *Encyclopaedia Britannica*, attempts after the Renaissance to rationalize the myth resulted in Atlantis' being identified variously with America, Scandinavia, the Canaries, or Palestine, and ethnologists saw in its inhabitants the ancestors of the Guanchos, the Basques, or the ancient Indians.

cal Society also believe in Atlantis, which figures in their scheme of human evolution, seven of the races of mankind having appeared during the fourth or Atlantean Epoch which preceded the present "Aryan" Epoch in this earth's history.

Atlantis was the Cradle of Mankind, the Garden of Eden, the Gardens of the Hesperides, the Elysian Fields, all the ideal commonwealths of ancient history. Lord Bacon sketched such an archetypal state in his literary fragment, *The New Atlantis*.

Mexican god, Quetzalcoatl, depicted in an ancient Indian manuscript as holding up the sea. Believers in the Lost Continent of Atlantis say that Quetzalcoatl and Atlas were the same deity, that both were Atlantean, and that this shows the Mexican Atlas supporting the world on his back. *After Lewis Spence.*

Atlantean gods were identified with the old deities of the Greeks, Phoenicians, Scandinavians, and Hindus; Atlantean religion was said to be a sun worship identical with that of Egypt and Peru. To the ancient continent were attributed all the great inventions of humankind, including metallurgy and the alphabet. Lewis Spence asserted in 1925 that Quetzalcoatl, the Mexican feathered serpent god, was also Atlas, and both were Atlantean, for "both were one of twins, both were magicians worshipped by tribes that practiced mummification, both were earth-bearers, both had maidens sacrificed to them by drowning, the Mayan girls being cast into the sacred cenote or well at Chichen Itza and the Canary Island ladies casting themselves into the sea as an offering to the god of ocean." The late Earnest Albert Hooton, professor of physical anthropology at Harvard, examined the skeletons from the Sacred Well at Chichen Itza and announced that thirteen were males, eight were adult or subadult females, seven were children aged ten to twelve, and fourteen were children six years old or less. They were unusually diseased in the the case of the adults, "somewhat inordinately battered," their skulls showing numerous lesions and fractures. "Altogether," observed Hooton, "it is suggested that the adult denizens of the Sacred Cenote may not have been generally beloved in their pre-sacrificial careers." Since all the sacred well legends related that only virgins were thrown in to become brides of the Rain God, Hooton noted further: "All of the individuals involved (or rather immersed) may have been virgins, but the osteological evidence does not permit a determination of this nice point."

Atlantis advocates seize on any faint resemblances, real or fancied, to support their theories, and if this evidence can somehow be phrased in the garb of science, as so many television commercials are presented today, it is considered proved, at least by the mystics. In 1883, W. S. Blacket, writing his *Researches into the Lost Histories of America,* noted gravely that the Guatemalan Quiche palace or temple which John L. Stephens had described in his charming *Incidents of Travel* was the identical structure Plato portrayed, and it was not until sixty-four years later that Tulane University excavations at Utatlan revealed that this Quiche capital was not built until the last great epoch of Maya history, after the beginning of the fifteenth century A.D., more than sixteen hundred years after Plato's death and over ten thousand years later than the date Atlantis devotees assign to the lost civilization.

Similarly, Atlantean theorists claimed ample geological support for a sunken land mass in the ocean between Europe and

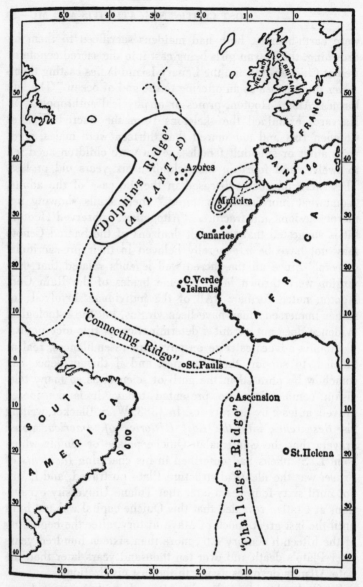

Map of the sunken Atlantis continent and its islands and ridges, from deep-sea soundings, according to Ignatius Donnelly.

America, although the geologists who unwittingly supplied the data had no such recent dates in mind as those attributed to its disappearance by Plato and his followers. One of the most telling chapters in Ignatius Donnelly's bestselling *Atlantis: The Antediluvian World*—the 1880 edition was its eighteenth printing—is that in which he combs the available geological and historical literature for cataclysms that radically altered the earth's surface within the memory of man. For example he quotes Winchell's *The Preadamites* to the effect that the entire South American coast lifted bodily ten or fifteen feet and let down again in an hour, and that the Andes sank two hundred and twenty feet in seventy years. Donnelly felt sure that the Atlantis subsidence was merely the last of a vast number of changes similar to that which he said submerged Britain to a depth of at least seventeen hundred feet and lifted it again from the ocean, by which Sicily was raised from beneath the waves to an elevation of three thousand feet, and the Sahara Desert brought up from a deposit of the sea. In 1783 a submarine volcano burst forth in the ocean thirty miles from Iceland, threw up an island of high cliffs which the King of Denmark immediately named and claimed, but within a year it sank again out of sight, leaving a reef thirty fathoms under water. In April, 1815, a volcanic eruption on an island two hundred miles east of Java was said to have destroyed all but twenty-six persons of a population of twelve thousand. On November 1, 1755, at Lisbon, a sound as of thunder was heard underground, and immediately after, an earthquake threw down the greater part of the city, killing sixty thousand persons in six minutes; a new marble quay there sank suddenly to a depth of six hundred feet, and the celebrated geographer, Alexander von Humboldt, stated that a portion of the earth's surface four times the size of Europe was simultaneously shaken. At Fez, Morocco, during the same quake, the ground opened, swallowed a village of ten thousand inhabitants, and closed again over them. Donnelly concludes:

These facts would seem to show that the great fires which destroyed Atlantis are still smouldering in the depths of the ocean; that the vast oscillations which carried Plato's continent beneath the sea may again bring it, with all its buried treasures, to the light; and that even the wild imagination of Jules Verne, when he described Captain Nemo, in his diving armor, looking down upon the temple and towers of the lost island, lit by the fires of submarine volcanoes, had some groundwork of possibility to build upon. . . . Who shall say that one hundred years from now the great museums of the world may not be adorned with gems, statues, arms, and implements from Atlantis, while the libraries of the world shall contain translations of its inscriptions, throwing new light upon all the past history of the human race, and all the great problems which now perplex the thinkers of our day?[3]

The Pacific counterpart of Atlantis is Lemuria, more commonly known as Mu—not to be confused with Le Plongeon's Queen Moo, which, if it is a Maya name, should rhyme with "toe"—another lost continent which produced a great civilization but is now, too, sunk beneath the all-devouring waves of ocean, as writers on these topics are prone to say it. James Churchward, its best-known historian, published his last book on Mu in 1931; the champions of each theory tolerate the other, presumably realizing that any telling arguments against one lost continent could be applied with equal effect against the other, but for a time there was some rivalry between them. An earlier Churchward, William, complained in a 3800-word letter to a Saturday edition of the *Brooklyn Times* in 1890 that everyone knows all about Atlantis; even children can plot its location and extent, he claimed, but "who can offhand draw the lines of Lemuria? It is just as much a continent as the famed Atlantis, but who knows its former place upon the

[3] Ignatius Donnelly had urged that the nations of the earth "employ their idle navies in bringing to the light of day some of the relics of this buried people." He argued that a single engraved tablet dredged from Plato's island "would be worth more to science, would more strike the imagination of mankind, than all the gold of Peru, all the monuments of Egypt, and all the terra-cotta fragments gathered from the great libraries of Chaldea." That was at least one statement on the subject that never incited argument.

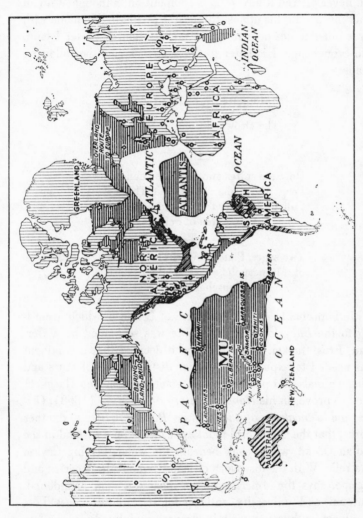

The Lost Continents of Mu, in the Pacific, and Atlantis, in the Atlantic, according to James Churchward.

globe?" Probably because Atlantis got off to an earlier start, Mu never offered it any serious competition, although William Churchward did his utmost to boost it by linking its name with three other topics dear to the mystics: Atlantis, Easter Island, and Stonehenge. His letter to the *Times* carried the following heads:

RELICS OF AN EXTINCT RACE

The Drowned Continent of the
Pacific Islands.

Only the spires and Points of Land Now
Peep Above the Waves But These Are
Full of Interest to Travelers and Spec-
tacled Men of Science.

Two sages, Plato of Athens and Donnelly
of Minneapolis, have made Atlantis a
household word.

Mu is probably a shortened form of Lemuria, which according to the *Encyclopedia Americana* was so named by a German, Ernst Jaekel, 1834–1919, who decided that a continent was needed to explain the peculiar distribution of lemurs and other animals and plants. Jaekel (sometimes spelled Haeckel) tried to prove, in his *Natural History of Creation* (1868), *Origin and Genealogy of the Human Race* (1870), and other works, that the Old World monkeys evolved on an island in the Indian Ocean, which sank beneath the water, leaving Ceylon as a relic. With the discovery of lemur remains in America and Europe, says the *Americana*, the idea was soon abandoned. Museum and university anthropologists, whose offices Lost Continent enthusiasts visit in droves, ruefully disagree. Jennings C. Wise, on the other hand, says that a Scotsman gave the Pacific continent the name Lemuria, from a Roman sacrificial festival dedicated to the ghosts "of the vanished worlds of their origin."

James Churchward followed the familiar patterns of thought and exposition that one comes to recognize among the least inhibited professional adventurers and pseudo-science writers. His personal narrative begins in India, where he says he was befriended by an old priest who saw him trying to decipher a bas-relief inscription one day. His priestly friend gave him lessons for two years in the dead language he believed to be the original tongue of mankind. Churchward finally persuaded the old man to show him some secret tablets which turned out to be the "genuine records of Mu." After translating these, and also over twenty-five hundred stones found by a man named William Niven in Mexico, Churchward studied the writings "of all the old civilizations"—something no single authoritative linguist has ever claimed to do—to compare them with Mu's legends, and he found that the Mu civilization preceded the Greek, Chaldean, Babylonian, Persian, Egyptian, and Hindu. Not only that, said the author, he learned the original story of creation, and it "was on the continent of Mu that man first came into being." From here on, the story has a most familiar ring: Colonizers from Mu settled in India, thence to Egypt, thence to the temple of Sinai—where Moses copied the story—and so on and on. One exasperated anthropologist wondered whether it would not be more reasonable to suppose that it was less the cataclysms of nature that wiped out these civilizations than a possible head-on clash between the eager colonizers of Mu and those of Atlantis.

For Churchward the great antiquity of the Naacal tablets, which he himself discovered, was sufficiently attested "by the fact that history says the Naacals left Burma more than 15,000 years ago." He cited no further authority or documentation or evidence for this remarkable statement; the age suggested puts the tablets well back into the Old Stone Age, some ten thousand years before writing was even invented according to most anthropologists. The Mexican tablets, said Churchward, are over twelve thousand years old; this would make them approximately contemporaneous with Tepexpan Man in the Valley of Mexico, an Ice Age hunter of now extinct mammoths, who, modern archeologists say, would have had some difficulty signing his name with an x. Discrepancies like this did not worry Churchward, who concluded that the Mexican record, like that of Naacal, "indubitably establishes to my own satisfaction that at one time the earth had an incalculably ancient civilization, which was, in many respects, superior to our own, and far in advance of us in some important essentials which the modern world is just beginning to have cognizance of.

The "Hieratic Alphabet" of Mu, from tablets allegedly discovered by James Churchward.

These tablets, with other ancient records, bear witness to the amazing fact that the civilizations of India, Babylonia, Persia, Egypt and Yucatan were but the dying embers of the first great civilization."

Churchward explained the crudeness of subsequent Stone Age archeological remains on the premise that prior to the destruction of Mu there had been no savagery, but when their great civilization died, the survivors did not know how to shift for themselves, managing to fashion only a few tools and weapons and some coarse foliage clothing, and were driven in cases to cannibalism in their fight for survival. "Savagery came out of civilization, not civilization out of savagery," he insisted. "It is only those who know nothing of savages who maintain that civilization emerged from savagery." This sort of talk is more than mildly annoying to anthropologists, the professional experts on savages. They audibly grit their teeth when Churchward further expounds, "A savage, left to himself does *not rise*. He has fallen to where he is and is still going down. It is only when he is brought into contact with civilization that an upward change in him becomes possible."

Churchward was not the first nor the last theorist along this line to invoke the unusual notion of cultural retrogression to explain how a civilization became less advanced than its great ancestor. Harold S. Gladwin in *Men Out of Asia* had the same thing happen after the great Mochica period in Peru, although most authorities deny any industrial degeneration at that stage of Andean prehistory. Thor Heyerdahl's *Kon-Tiki* theory explains the absence of Peruvian traits in Polynesia as due to stagnation and retrogression which became "natural" in an island environment—a complete reversal, as the anthropologist Edward Norbeck pointed out, of Heyerdahl's argument elsewhere that it was most improbable that migrants from Indonesia or Asia would lose such crafts as pottery-making and weaving in a move eastward into the Pacific. Lady Richmond Brown, F.L.S., F.R.G.S., F.Z.S., in a final chapter of "Observations and Analysis" in her travel adventure book, *Unknown Tribes, Unchartered Seas*, brings up the Lost Continent of Atlantis and asks, "Is it not possible that a mighty empire existed, probably far greater than our own, covering millions of square miles of territory which are now deep beneath the ocean—that some remnants of a stupendous annihilation survived, and that these primitive tribes to-day are the descendants, sinking ever downwards by a process of devolution, from their once high estate?" In 1817, James H. McCulloh, M.D., wrote, "For my part, I believe that unless man had been created civilized, he would never have risen to it by his own exertions;—we see, when left to ourselves, how degraded we are." Finally, Dr. Samuel Kirkland Lothrop, distinguished anthropologist of the Peabody Museum of Harvard, asked sarcastically: "Why do the group of writers who would derive New World culture from the Old—be it Atlantis, Mu, Asia, or the Four Corners—always find subsequent degeneration? Is it psychic unity?"

Churchward learned much more about Mu through his "translations" of the secret tablets than anyone ever claimed to know about Atlantis, even Plato. His scenes of Mu are idyllic. "Over the cool river, gaudy-winged butterflies hovered in the shade of trees, rising and falling in fairy-like movement, as if better to view their painted beauty in nature's mirror. Darting hither and thither from flower to flower, hummingbirds made their short flights, glistening like living jewels in the rays of the sun. Feathered songsters in bush and tree vied with each other in their sweet lays." He pictured in great detail almost every aspect of life on Mu; how it all got on the secret tablets is a marvel. Population: "The great continent was teeming with gay and happy life over which 64,000,000 human beings reigned supreme. All this life was rejoicing in its luxuriant home." Race: "The dominant race in the land of Mu was a white race, exceedingly handsome people, with clear white or olive skins, large, soft, dark eyes and straight black hair." Navigation: "On cool evenings might be seen pleasure ships, filled with gorgeously dressed, jewel-bedecked men and women. The long sweeps with which these ships were supplied gave a musical rhythm to the song and laughter of the happy passengers." Since there was apparently no mention of steamships or outboard motors on Mu, these oars were presumably manned by somewhat less joyously blissful galley slaves, probably not of the "dominant race."

A quite different picture of Mu—or Lemuria—is offered by Max Heindel in his *Rosicrucian Cosmo-Conception,* published in 1929. According to Heindel, whose announced intention was to reconcile the apparently conflicting mystic cosmologies of the famous Theosophist, Mme H. P. Blavatsky, and of another revered occultist, A. P. Sinnett, author of *Esoteric Buddhism,* the Lemurian epoch was long ago when the earth's crust was just beginning to harden, some of it still fiery, with seas of boiling water between the islands. The atmosphere was

"dense"—somewhat like the fire-fog of a previous Moon period—the forms of man and animal were yet "quite plastic."
The skeleton had formed, all right, but man had the power of
molding his flesh and that of the animals about him. He had
no eyes, only two sensitive spots which were affected by the
light of the sun "as it shone dimly through the fiery atmosphere of ancient Lemuria." His language consisted of sounds
"like those of Nature," derived from the wind sighing in the

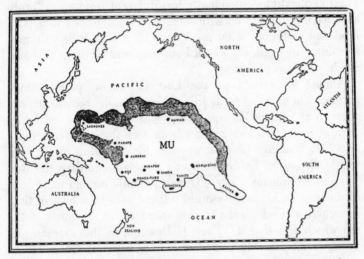

The Lost Continent of Mu, according to James Churchward

super-tropical forest, from rippling brooks, howling tempests,
thundering waterfalls, and the volcano's roar.

It was possible to see only a few feet in any direction, wrote
Heindel, and the outline of all objects not close at hand appeared dim, hazy, and uncertain. "Man was guided more by
internal perception than by external vision," he explained.
The inhabitant of Atlantis had a head, but scarcely any fore-
head; his brain had no frontal development; the head sloped
almost abruptly back from a point just above the eyes. "Instead of walking, he progressed by a series of flying leaps, not

unlike those of the kangaroo. He had small blinking eyes and his hair was round in section. . . . The ears of the Atlantean sat much farther back upon the head than do those of the Aryan. . . ." Claude Falls Wright, whose 1894 expositions of modern theosophy followed closely those of a Theosophical Society's founder, Mme Blavatsky, states that Lemurians were said to be twenty-seven to thirty feet high and to have possessed powers of nature that we cannot conceive of today. Their civilization consequently was different from ours, "probably having more to do with science and philosophy than with food and clothing." That must have been a blessing to a person thirty feet tall, for whom both food and clothing could be a fairly serious problem.

Almost all writers on the Lost Continents picture them shrouded in swirling mist. In the Max Heindel reconstruction, Atlantis as well as Mu was murky with it, "surrounded by an aura of light-mist, like a street lamp seen through dense fog." In 1931, Jennings C. Wise wrote in his *Red Man in the New World Drama* of Fabre d'Olivet's theories regarding the Red Race as Atlanteans. "For d'Olivet, Atlantis was no mere land of dreams. To his incisive mind it lifted out of the haze of time as clearly as he believed it once stood above the mists of the sea which engulfed it." Even Hollywood, in its caveman pictures, seems compelled to blow dry ice vapors from cracks in the ground and induce low clouds to drift across the sets.

Not all of those who have succumbed to the tropical fever of Lost Continents and Egypt-in-America have been uneducated, unintelligent, or unscrupulous cranks. Less than a century ago, the malady claimed one of the world's most respected scholars. From the age of seventeen, when he was intrigued by a report in the *Gazette de France* that a Brazilian farmer had found a flat stone, Macedonian arms and armor, all bearing Greek inscriptions, Charles Stephen Brasseur de Bourbourg had devoted his life to the study of American antiquities. Thirty years later, a famed authority on Mexican Indian history, language, and culture, he became depressed and frustrated with doubt and cynicism. Discounting all his previous conclusions about native archeology and history, he made a decision that the historian Hubert Howe Bancroft later called "a sacrifice of labor unique . . . in the annals of literature."

Born in 1814 in a small town in the north of France, Brasseur felt, as he put it, "a lively interest in all geographical facts relating to America" after he read the account of the alleged Grecian remains in Brazil. A subsequent article in the *Journal des Savants* by Antonio del Río, an artillery captain

Charles Stephen Brasseur de Bourbourg. *After Winsor, courtesy of the Library of Congress.*

who explored the now famous Maya ruins of Palenque, decided for Brasseur his archeological calling, although for a brief period at age twenty-one he first tried his hand, with small success, at writing romances and moral tales, the first of these entitled *Les Épreuves de la Fortune et d'Adversité*. Then he turned to philosophical and theological studies, traveled in Germany, Italy, and Sicily, and in 1845 took holy orders and came to America.

Here at last he was in the homeland of the native Indian cultures and tribes that were to claim his attention for the rest of his days. Boston, he once wrote, "will never cease to be especially dear to my memory," for there he first became acquainted with American Indian prehistory through the famous writings of William H. Prescott, whose *Conquest of Mexico* is still the classic work on Cortez and his conquistadores. To discharge his priestly duties, Brasseur taught church history for a year in the Catholic Seminary in Quebec, then returned to Rome to represent the Catholic Church of North America at the papal court of Pius IX. He made no secret of the fact, however, that his main interest was always less in religious matters than in the American aboriginal culture. "I am an abbé of the church," he remarked to a North American admirer who met him in Rome, "but my ecclesiastical duties have always rested very lightly upon me."

This admitted devotion to archeology led him again and again to seek church assignments that would further his Indian studies. He was happy in Rome because it afforded him an opportunity to consult the rare Mexican codices and other native Indian documents treasured in the Vatican. But he could not long stay away from America, and in 1848 he was back again, visited New York and Niagara, and retraced the old French explorers' routes down the Mississippi to New Orleans. From there he took passage for Veracruz, Mexico, to become "almoner of the French Legation" but actually to devote more intense firsthand study to Mexican Indian languages, customs, history, and antiquities. He was still in Mexico when he began to experience his astonishing intellectual reversal.

The famed Abbé Brasseur, after years of travel seeking out long-forgotten Indian documents, of painfully pouring over the dim scrawling inscriptions, and piecing together the story of the Mexican past into a meaningful history, had gradually begun to suspect something entirely new and very disturbing about his records. Deep in his mind, at first almost subconsciously, but later gnawing at him with an ever more urgent insistence, grew a doubt that the ancient Toltecs, the predecessors of the Aztecs and the conquerors of the Maya of Yucatan, about whom he had written so many learned tomes, had ever existed at all! To his own horror he became increasingly convinced that all these native writings which he had so laboriously translated from the original Nahuatl and Yucatec Maya and Guatemalan Quiche were in fact pure allegory, and that the deities and other mythological characters of Maya and Mexican legends, to whose understanding he had contributed more than any man alive, were simply Indian representations of the great forces of nature. But what forces of nature?

Perplexed, then bewildered by the strange and complex writings of a past civilization whose concepts and habits of thought he could not fathom, the Abbé turned in desperation, as so many of us do in times of stress, to the unreal world, to supernaturalism, for the answers. It was typical of Brasseur that once convinced that he was right, there was no turning back. In his Mexican study, so far from his beloved Paris and his even more beloved Rome, he now seized his old-fashioned turkey-quill pen, dipped it in a bottle of homemade red-brown ink, and carefully scratched the first lines of the book *Quatre Lettres*, that was to turn his scientific admirers against him to a man and ruin a reputation for scholarship that he had so laboriously built in years of travel, study, and writing.

Once freed of empirical requirements, of the demands of science, he found answers readily enough, as do all mystics. Things suddenly became very clear. The pyramids of Egypt were like those of Mexico, they must be related. How? Well, they must have descended from some common ancestral civilization. Atlantis! If Atlantis was the mother of all great cultures, it would explain the many resemblances between Egypt and ancient Mexico. American prehistoric civilizations must have originated on Atlantis, colonists from that continent having settled in America and thus, like the Guanchos, their alleged countrymen of the Canary Islands, escaped the disaster that befell their homeland. This Atlantean race, said Brasseur, spread from the New World and created the Egyptian and other great civilizations of the Old. The Egyptian god, Horus, was none other than Quetzalcoatl, the Mexican-Maya feathered-serpent god. Other ancient American deities were actually the great Nature forces that destroyed Atlantis. He wrote on and on and on; his ideas, no longer bridled by scientific caution and reason, stampeded down the precipitous road of mysticism.

Brasseur was held in such great regard that most archeological and historical authorities of the time, although disagreeing wholly with his latest views and greatly disturbed by this turn of events in his scholarly life, were unwilling to condemn him publicly. The Abbé lived ten years after he announced his startling new theories, years of considerable loneliness, sorrow, and of determined obstinacy in his beliefs. In their defense he attempted a translation of a famous Indian manuscript, the *Troano,* but by now emotion ruled his mind, and his conclusions became wilder and wilder, his writings rambling and disconnected, until he died, grief-stricken over the rejection of his theories and humiliated by the eloquent silence with which they were received. The historian Bancroft wrote shortly after the Abbé's death in 1874:

Brasseur de Bourbourg devoted his life to the study of American primitive history. In actual knowledge pertaining to his chosen subjects, no man ever equalled or approached him. In the last decade of his life, he conceived a new and complicated theory respecting the origin of the American people, or rather the origin of

Europeans and Asiatics from America, made known to the world in his *"Quatre Lettres."* By reason of the extraordinary nature of the views expressed, and the author's well-known tendency to build magnificent structures on a slight foundation, his later writings were received, for the most part by critics utterly incompetent to understand them, with a sneer, or what seems to have grieved the writer more, in silence. Now that the great Americanist is dead, while it is not likely that his theories will ever be received, his zeal in the cause of antiquarian science, and the many valuable works of his pen will be better appreciated.

LOST TRIBES
AND THE MORMONS

THE LOST TRIBES OF ISRAEL! Who can fail
to be intrigued by these words, which have a familiar ring
even though we may have only the vaguest comprehension of
the theory. Perhaps we remember hazily that the Israelites
were conquered by an enemy king somewhere back in Old Testament times and that some of them were said to be "lost"—
wandered or were carried away to disappear from history. The
theory that the Lost Tribes found their way to America and
were responsible for a number of the ancient Indian civilizations here has claimed many a devotee, including one renowned
scholar who gave his fortune and then his life to this magnificent obsession.

Edward King, the young Viscount Kingsborough, firstborn
heir of an Irish earl, was strolling idly through the Bod-
leian Library at Oxford one grey, foggy morning early in
the nineteenth century. News of Andrew Jackson's victory over
British troops on the bloody Chalmette floodplain near New
Orleans had just reached England, and like many of his fellow
students at Exeter College the young Lord Kingsborough was
bitter, disillusioned about politics and government, and in

search of some more rewarding outlet for his intellectual interests and his considerable wealth. Armed with a note of introduction which gave him access to the rarest items of the priceless collections, he stopped for a moment in front of a dusty case containing an ancient Mexican Indian manuscript, painted by the natives with vegetable and mineral pigments on stiff, white-plastered deerskin. Its bold colors were still clear after at least three hundred years, and the strange art style and grotesque depictions so foreign to Western European culture immediately caught his eye. Fascinated, King bent low over this ancient codex, lost to surroundings and oblivious to the passing time. Quite literally his discovery was to lead to his untimely death.

The young man fell in love with Mexican antiquities at this very moment, and it became the ruling obsession of his ill-fated life. On completing his studies at Oxford he was elected to the House of Commons (his peerage title was held by courtesy only), but there was not room in his life for both activities: it was American antiquities all or nothing. He did not seek re-election as a member of Parliament, but instead retired from public life completely to study Mexican manuscripts and archeology.

In the course of his readings, Kingsborough, whose allegiances were apparently of the most violent kind, became passionately convinced that the Mexican Indians were descendants of the "Lost Tribes of Israel," ten, or as some say, nine and a half tribes of the ancient kingdom that were conquered and carried away from Samaria by the king of Assyria in 721 B.C., leaving behind the tribes of Judah, Benjamin, and the half tribe of Menasseh. According to some proposals, the Hebrews reached Central and South America directly from the Eastern Hemisphere, but most supporters of the Lost Tribes theory feel that the route was across Persia, the frontiers of China, and Bering Strait. At any rate, Lord Kingsborough went so far overboard with his obsession that in spite of his father's great financial difficulties, he spent his entire remaining fortune assembling and publishing a magnificent set of nine imperial folio volumes reproducing Mexican codices and commenting on Mexican antiquities, a collector's item today, but a luxury that put him, four years after the first of them appeared, in arrears with a paper manufacturer in the amount £508 10s. 6d.

In 1835, it will be remembered, people still went to prison for debt, and in November of that year London society had a choice scandal for their favorite pastime of gossiping: this once wealthy nobleman was imprisoned in a common debtor's prison, doubtless to the smug satisfaction of those who had openly disapproved when he had earlier renounced his birthright. Kingsborough stayed in the sheriff's jail until December 4, but just short of a year later, on October 1, 1836, he returned for eleven days on a similar conviction: this time for a debt of £26 4s. 11d. On his release, his friends thought that he must at last have learned his lesson, that he would now buckle down and forget the frivolities of his intellectual passion, gain solvency, and stay out of trouble. But Edward King was fatally addicted to his particular favorite drug. He kept up the luxury publishing, and within a month began a third prison term, for a debt of £118 17s. 7d. He died in debtor's prison a year later, at the age of forty-two, accounts conflicting as to whether it was from typhus, typhoid fever, or, as some maintained, a broken heart. Jacinto Jijón e Caamaño, who wrote a memorial to him in 1918, says that if Lord Kingsborough had lived one more year he would have inherited the titles and prerogatives of his father, together with a rental income of £40,000 annually. We learn to count on the historian, Hubert Howe Bancroft, to appraise a man's best and worst qualities. Although Bancroft had little patience with the Lost Tribes theory, and although he stated readily that the Viscount lacked impartiality and profound research, that his data were far from orderly as presented, and that Kingsborough was a fanatic, nevertheless his enthusiasm was never offensive. "There is a scholarly dignity about his work which has never been attained by those who have jeered and railed at him; and though we may smile at his credulity, and regret that such strong zeal was so strangely misplaced, yet we should speak and think with respect of one who spent his lifetime and his fortune, if not his reason, in an honest endeavor to cast light upon one of the most obscure spots in the history of man."

This unfortunate young man was not the first nor by many thousands the last person to believe that American Indians were remnants of the Israelites. There were many Lost Tribes writings in the sixteenth and seventeenth centuries,[1] for a number of Spaniards in America were glad to have an excuse to relegate the aborigines to the miserable status of the European Jews. Just how much logic was demanded of scholars in those days is indicated by a passage from the Amsterdam rabbi, Menasseh ben Israel's celebrated *Origin de los Americanos, esto es esperanza de Israel*, published in 1650. It told of a Jewish traveler in South America, a man named Aaron Levi, alias Antonio Montesini, who was sure that his Indian guide was an Israelite when the latter greeted him with the Shema (Shema Israel, "Hear, O Israel," Deut. 4:4). When the guide assured Montesini that a considerable number of Indians "of the same origin" as himself lived in the mountains near Quito, Montesini and the Chief Rabbi of Amsterdam after him jumped to the conclusion that a lost tribe of Israelites still lived in the South American highland.

[1] Bartolomé de las Casas, the Spanish priest who so stoutly championed Indian rights in an era when exploitation of the natives was accepted procedure, was said by Father Torquemada to have been the first to suggest the theory over four hundred years ago, but as Edward John Payne of University College pointed out in 1899, the evidence that Torquemada offered in defense of this supposition actually argued against it.

According to a great authority on Hebrew history, Allen H. Godbey, one of the earliest Lost Tribes backers was another Spaniard of the early sixteenth century, Francisco López de Gomara, as were a French Calvinist, De Lecy, Genebrard, and Andrew Thevel of roughly the same period. J. Imbelloni adds to these the name of Diego Gonzalo Fernández Oviedo (1535). Dr. Godbey mentions Father Duran, whose famous *Historia de las Indias de Nueva España* appeared in 1585. Gregorio García also wrote about this hypothesis in the latter part of the century. Among the host of Lost Tribes advocates who came along in succeeding generations were Roger Williams, John Eliot, William Penn, Samuel Sewall, and Increase and Cotton Mather.

Other early writers preached that to discover the long-lost tribes, after more than two thousand years still under the special protection of Almighty God though despised by all mankind, would "lead all men to the acknowledgment, that the God of Israel, is a God of truth and righteousness, and that whom he loves, he loves unto the end." Since anthropology as a science was non-existent in those days, the missionaries, historians, and other travelers exploring the rapidly expanding known world were constantly amazed at similarities they found in ways of life between hitherto unknown tribes and those already familiar to them through biblical stories. Today you can go to the Human Relations Area Files at any one of many universities, ask for an inventory of all the peoples of the world who practice some particular custom—preferred cousin marriage, say—and in a relatively short time you can have all the known examples, together with the detailed data and history of each. Early writers, though, unaware of how similar customs can develop independently of each other, were usually inclined to attribute them to historical connections.

The ancient Hebrew tribal culture was the best known in those times, its "strange" ways (marriage by purchase or in return for services to the father-in-law, inheritance of a widowed sister-in-law as one's wife, human and animal sacrifice, and so on) being familiar through Old Testament stories of Abraham, Isaac, Jacob, Rachel, Laban, Leah, Bilha & Company. When their supposedly unique customs began to turn up elsewhere in the world, particularly in view of the many prophecies that the Jews would some day return and be reunited with their brethren, pious travelers discovered lost Israelite remnants among the Afghans, Abyssinians, African Masai and Zulus, Kaffirs, Japanese, Burmese, Karens, and Malays; even the old Anglo-Saxons, once their customs were known to literary historians, became Hebrew by descent. The American Indians of course joined this illustrious company in due time, for here and there among them one could hardly escape seeing first-fruit ceremonies, new fire festivals, sacrifices to gods, lunar and ritual calendars, legends of destroying giants, flood myths, feasts, exorcisms, purification rites, fasting and food taboos, confession, pilgrimages, endogamy and other marriage restrictions, and above all, circumcision and the veneration of a tribal Ark.

According to an early eighteenth-century player of this particular gamesmanship, fifteen hundred years after Joshua expelled the Canaanites, his descendants, having discovered their origin and animated by their ancient hatred, fought the battle of Jericho all over again on American soil, this time burning their New World temples, towers and cities. Lescarbot concluded that the New World was peopled not by Israelites, but by the Canaanites whom the former had themselves expelled. He stated flatly that Americans are descendants of Noah. Josiah Priest, in his *American Antiquities* (1798), attempted to show that America was settled before the flood; that it was the country of Noah, and the place where the ark was erected. However, Priest said that the famous Indian mounds at Marietta, on the Ohio River, were the ruins of a Roman fort.

Dissenters to the theory were not long in making themselves heard. In 1633, William Wood, after a short visit to New England, protested that American Indian words, which had been declared related to Hebrew, might as well be considered the gleanings of all nations, "because they have words which sound after the Greek, Latin, French, and other tongues. . . ." In 1652, Sir Hamon L'Estrange wrote a treatise entitled *Americans no Jewes*, and the Israelite theory was further opposed by J. Ogilby in 1670, and by Hubbard, who wrote in his 1680 *History of New England:* "If any observation be made of their manners and dispositions, it's easier to say from what nations they did not, than from whom they did, derive their origin. Doubtless their conjecture who fancy them to be descended from the ten tribes of Israelites . . . hath the least show of reason of any other, there being no footsteps to be observed of their propinquity to them more than to any other of the tribes of the earth, either as to their language or manners." Père

Leveque in 1836 recognized the pitfalls in Lost Tribes reasoning: "If Julius Caesar had been a lover of the Jews," he wrote, "or if he felt, in any way, interested in their affairs he could equally well have discovered the lost tribes of Israel among the ancient Gauls and Britains in his Bellum Gallicum."

John MacKintosh, who translated Leveque's work, attacked the Lost Tribes theory most vigorously in his own book the same year, warning that superficial resemblance between the sounds of Hebrew words and those of various Indian languages was not enough on which to propose historical connection; "the judgments of those who endeavoured to make researches this way, were so much perverted that resemblances were imagined which had no existence in reality." In 1853, Mariano Edward Rivero and John James von Tschudi, writing on Peruvian antiquities, devoted several pages to evidence then thought to favor the Israelite theory, but concluded that the hypothesis "rests on no solid foundation."

By mid-nineteenth century another line of argument was being applied against the Lost Tribes idea of Indian origins. James Kennedy, Esq., LL.B., writing on the *Probable Origin of the American Indians, with Particular Reference to That of the Caribs,* observed that the ten tribes were never lost at all. In 1872 John D. Baldwin declared that there was not anywhere a fact, a suggestion, or a circumstance of any kind to show that the ten tribes ever left southwest Asia, where they dwelt after the destruction of their kingdom. "They were 'lost' to the Jewish nation because they rebelled, apostatised, and, after their subjugation by the Assyrians in 721 B.C., were to a great extent absorbed by other peoples in that part of Asia. Some of them were probably still in Palestine when Christ appeared. This wild notion, called a theory, scarcely deserves so much attention." This point of view is held today by leading Hebrew scholars; in his definitive book, *The Lost Tribes a Myth,* Dr. A. H. Godbey, professor of Old Testament at Duke University, complained that the fancy is still expounded from the pulpit by men supposed to be scholars, who "hold up the political disappearance of the 'lost tribes' as an awful illustration of the punishment of individual sinfulness; as though becoming an American were the penalty for being a sinful Englishman."

To anthropologists, the most famous Lost Tribes advocate, besides Lord Kingsborough, was James Adair, who lived for forty years among the North American Indians during the latter half of the eighteenth century. As Samuel G. Drake declared in 1841, Adair "tormented every custom and usage into a like one of the Jews, and almost every word in their language became a Hebrew one of the same meaning." For example, Adair said that during Indian first-fruit ceremonies the natives chanted the mystic phrase, *Yo Meschica, He Meschica, Va Meschica*; to a fervent supporter of the Israelite theory the first syllables of these three terms formed the name Jehovah, and the rest of each term was clearly Messiah. Adair supported his contention both coming and going, so to speak; when he heard the Indians chant *Schiluhyu, Schiluhe, Schiluhva*, he chose the last syllables this time to see again Jehovah, the Schiluh being the same as Hebrew Scheleach or Schiloth, "messenger or pacificator." The Indians called an accused or guilty person *Haksit canaha*; this, Adair assured his readers, means "a sinner of Canaan." How Canaanites reached America is another long involved story, supported by another long list of people, including the French scholar, Lescarbot, an advocate of the Parliament of Paris, in 1611, and President Esra Stiles of Yale (1783).

The late Theodore A. Willard, manufacturer of batteries, was an enthusiast on Maya antiquities who looked favorably on the Lost Tribes theory as well as the Atlantis myth. He recalled Bishop Diego de Landa's sixteenth-century account of an old Yucatec tradition that their first settlers had come from the east by water—a legend almost invariably cited as evidence by supporters of the Phoenician, Egyptian, Israelite, and Atlantis theories—and he called attention to the "distinctly Semitic cast of countenance" on human figures depicted in ancient sculptures and murals of Maya ruins. "The dignity of

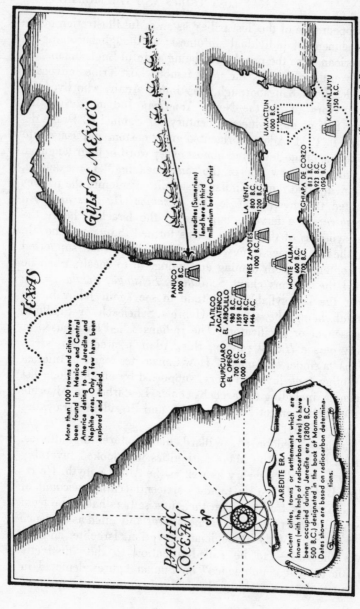

(Courtesy T. S. Ferguson).

The Jaredite Era in Mormon belief. Sumerian Jaredites landed on the Gulf Coast of Mexico and founded the centers which are now ancient ruins.

face and serene poise of these carved or painted likenesses," he wrote in 1926, "is strikingly Hebraic."

Contrary to popular belief, and indeed contradicting many a standard encyclopedia, the Church of Jesus Christ of Latter-day Saints denies that their *Book of Mormon* is concerned with the Lost Tribes, but it has been the most active and persistent organization seeking to prove that Hebrews came to America and founded here the Indian civilizations of pre-Columbian times, as recorded in their sacred book. For nineteen years young Mormon missionaries have visited my Tulane University office, some of them en route to the Gulf of Mexico and the Caribbean in hope of finding concrete support of the Mormon contention. One, with an explorer's beard and a gold ring in one ear lobe, skippered a schooner to the Gulf and planned to set adrift there a little fleet of scale models of the sailing craft described in *The Book of Mormon*. He would trace them by means of colored stains they were to release automatically as they floated over the waters, to find which segment of the main-land the ancient seafarers from Israel were likely to have reached first as they were carried along by prevailing winds and currents. I never saw this young man again, but from a description of him, his silken beard and gold earring, which I heard a year or so later, I judge that I missed a second visit from him. I should like to hear the results of his experiment.

So far as I know, the American Indian is not mentioned in any other official church dogma. Article 8, Chapter 15, of the *Articles of Faith for the Book of Mormon* presents the Church's evidence for its belief that America was settled by people called Jaredites who came direct from the confused scenes at the Tower of Babel as described in Genesis; that the Jaredites, after a series of calamities, were destroyed in the second cen-tury B.C.; and that an Israelite named Lehi and his followers also came to this continent from Jerusalem about 600 B.C., splitting into two groups, the Nephites and the Lamanites, the former building the great pre-Columbian cities of Middle America and the Andes, becoming extinct about A.D. 324; the

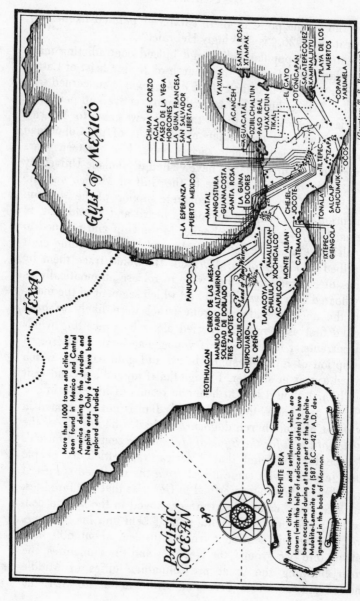

(Courtesy T. S. Ferguson)

The Nephite Era in Mormon belief. Israelites came to America about 600 B.C., one group of them, the Nephites, occupying the ancient cities shown on the map.

latter, a nomadic non-agricultural people who continued in a "degenerate condition," are now represented by the Indian tribes with which we in North America are more familiar.

L. A. Bertrand's *Mémoires d'un Mormon* gives a somewhat different account of Mormon beliefs: The Jaredites crossed the ocean in eight vessels, landed in North America, and built there some highly civilized nations and large cities; their descendants defied the Lord, however, and were destroyed six hundred years before Christ. Jerusalem Israelites replaced them, landing on the west coast of South America; also some descendants of Judah came from Jerusalem to North America, then emigrated to the northern parts of South America. The first Israelite group separated into two nations: the first named for the prophet Nephi, who led them to America, and the second named for their wicked and corrupt chief, Laman. The Nephites went to northern South America; the Lamanites occupied the central and southern parts of the same continent. The Nephites spread east, west, and north, prospered greatly, but were constantly warring with the pagan Lamanites. The Judah descendants also became atheistic and semi-barbaric, but learned the sacred scriptures from the Nephites, who joined them and later colonized the northern continent. Eventually the Nephites, too, fell from grace and were punished by earthquakes, fire from heaven, and war. Christ appeared to the Nephite remnants, and his apostles preached the gospel throughout the hemisphere, converting Nephites and Lamanites alike. They backslid again, though, and were "once more smitten by the arm of the Almighty." The Nephites perished in a great final battle near the hill of Cumorah (in New York state), where Mormon buried the sacred tablets eventually removed in 1827 by Joseph Smith.

President John Taylor of the Mormons said that the Mexican-Maya god, Quetzalcoatl-Kukulkan, and Christ were the same being, citing Lord Kingsborough's observation that Quetzalcoatl is depicted in Indian art as a person crucified. Two current Mormon writers, Milton R. Hunter and Thomas

Stuart Ferguson, present their additional reasons for supporting this belief, citing parallels between the descriptions of Quetzalcoatl in an early Mexican document and those in *The Book of Mormon*. They also call attention to Revelations 22:16, "I, Jesus, have sent mine angel to testify unto you these things in the churches. I am the root and offspring of David, and the bright and morning star." Quetzalcoatl was identified with Venus, the Morning Star, by his Indian worshippers; as a matter of fact, the crucifixion Lord Kingsborough noted is the widespread Morning Star sacrifice, a ritual in which a human being, often a slave or captive, was spread-eagled on a scaffold and then shot to death with an arrow. (Previous theorists on American Indian origins have identified Quetzalcoatl variously as Atlas, St. Thomas, Votan, Osiris, Dionysius, Bacchus, a Buddhist or Brahmin missionary, Viracocha and Mango Capac of Peru, Poseidon, and Hotu Matua, the culture hero of Easter Island in the Pacific.)

The Mormons rely on what they consider significant parallels between *The Book of Mormon* and the *Annals of Ixtlilxochitl,* the latter a historical document written in the sixteenth century by a Mexican Indian, Fernando de Alva Ixtlilxochitl, grandson of the last native king of Tezcuco. Hunter and Ferguson document this argument with descriptions and illustrations showing resemblances between the costumes, arts, crafts, architecture, and other cultural traits of the Egyptians, on the one hand, and the descendants of the Hebrews in America, on the other. They attack the orthodox anthropological "all-or-none" attitudes: that American Indians were all-Mongoloid-or-none racially, and that the New World was peopled all-by-way-of-Siberia-Bering-Strait-or-none. "Further, to claim that such bearded convex-nosed characters [depicted in Mexican and Yucatec remains] . . . are representatives of Mongoloids is to ignore clear-cut 'real evidence' to the contrary. They are representations of Caucasians and all the dodging and ignoring that is going on with respect to such evidence will not change the truth. . . . Those who persist in following the 'all-or-none' theories must accuse Ixtlilxochitl, Sahagún, Torquemada, the Señores of Totonicapan and Xahila, and Joseph Smith with ignorance or deliberate misstatements for saying that the colonizers came to America by boat from across the sea. These remarkable people are dead and cannot speak for themselves; however, the stone and ceramic figurines of the ancient colonizers are speaking quite eloquently out of the ground. They are 'voices from the dust' which constitute real evidence that will not easily be overcome; and, to a marked degree, it seems that this 'real evidence' points to the fact that the original settlers of Bountiful-land were very much like the ancient Near Easterners, both in mien and dress."

Since the *Annals* were not published in English until 1848— eighteen years after the first edition of *The Book of Mormon*— members of the Church of Jesus Christ of Latter-day Saints point out that the resemblances between the two books cannot be attributed to any knowledge Joseph Smith might have had of the Indian chronicle. Gentile critics of Mormonism, however, maintain that by 1830, when Smith published his translation of the gold tablets, there were numerous books on the Lost Tribes theory which he could have read and which could have influenced him in his rendering of the sacred inscriptions. They also feel that in 1600 or thereabouts, when Ixtlilxochitl was writing, he was doubtless strongly influenced by Christian instruction, which would have tinged his stories of Indian creation, the flood, the ark, a Babel-type tower, and a confusion of tongues with subsequent scattering of populations.

About a century ago, Lucien de Rosny pointed out resemblances between the Hebrew Bible and the Guatemala Quiche Indian sacred book, *Popol Vuh*, a collection of traditions and history written down soon after the Spanish conquest by one or more Quiche Indians. De Rosny showed that both Bibles contain a story of the sea parting miraculously to let fugitive tribes pass; both tell of a confusion of tongues and a Tower of Babel; and both relate how sacred law was handed down to priests on a mountain top, the Maya god, Tohil, giving it to his priest, Chi-Pixab, just as Jehovah gave it to Moses. It is also easy to find deluge stories and pictures in these native Indian books, even the clearly pre-Columbian Maya codices. Anthropologists attribute the almost identical passages of the *Popol Vuh* and the Bible to European influence on the native scribe who recorded the former, and they write off the pre-Columbian flood stories as independent legends stemming from different floods.

The late Professor Roland B. Dixon of Harvard included a discussion of deluge stories in his book, *The Building of Cultures*, which was devoted largely to attacking the Egyptianist diffusion school. Dixon said that myths recounting a great flood in which all persons were destroyed except one or a small group of survivors are widely distributed over the world, although less common in Africa than elsewhere. However, "apart from the basic idea of a flood from which but few escape, the details and even the fundamental ideas of the tales are different." In one case, he shows, the flood's cause may be an accident, in another it is due to divine displeasure, in another to personal enmity between two supernatural beings. "The means of safety may be a boat, or by climbing a tall tree or a mountain; the world may again become habitable by a recession of the waters, or may need to be re-created by the survivor." Dixon said that all peoples except those of the most arid regions must at one time or another have experienced sudden disastrous floods, and upon this, "mythic fancy builds its individual plot."

At Brigham Young University in Provo, Utah, a large department of archeology publishes its own *Bulletin*, the results of faculty and student research in this field. Some of the articles are straight factual reporting; some carry at least a brief interpretation favorable to Church dogma. The *Bulletin* has brought out some valuable trait distribution studies, concentrated on motifs that the Church finds relevant to its history. For example, in a 1953 issue, two articles are devoted to the "Tree of Life" depictions in Maya art. These are cross-shaped motifs that figure in a number of ancient Maya and Mexican sculptures and paintings in books. Regarding this figure as Christ's cross, early writers saw in it evidence that Christian teachings had reached the New World before Columbus. Modern archeologists usually refer to it as a conventionalized tree, which apparently figures in pre-Columbian mythology, history, or religion. To Mormons the various elements that appear fairly consistently in this motif not only indicate historical connection with the Old World, which has produced very similar art forms particularly in Java and Cambodia, but also are identified with familiar stories in the Bible and in Greek mythology.

Stylized tree in bas-relief sculpture, Temple of the Cross, Palenque, Mexico. Early Spaniards thought it was Christ's cross. The Mormons believe it represents the Tree of Life. *After A. P. Maudslay.*

Another work that is most interesting for its trait distributions, and by far the most comprehensive statement of evidence favoring Mormon beliefs about ancient America, is Thomas Stuart Ferguson's *One Fold and One Shepherd*, published in 1958. Its theme is that Central America and Mexico received their very early high civilization from Mesopotamian Jaredites who landed on the Gulf Coast of eastern Mexico in the third millennium B.C., and from two small groups of Israelites, descendants of Joseph, who crossed the ocean in the sixth century B.C., and that *The Book of Mormon* tells the history of this Hebrew colony from the time of its departure from Jerusalem in 597 B.C. until the destruction of its American nation in A.D. 385. Ferguson reminds us that *The Book of Mormon* does not purport to explain the origin of all cultures in all epochs and in all zones of the Western Hemisphere—only the high civilizations—and that it does not contradict the presence of Stone Age cultures is America prior to or during the period of which it treats, nor the possible influences from southeast Asia that we shall describe in chapter 6. *One Fold and One Shepherd*, representing a tremendous amount of work and study by its conscientious and devoted author, assembles numerous resemblances between Mexican-Maya archeological remains and documents on the one hand, and of "Bible lands" (chiefly Egypt, Asia Minor, and Mesopotamia) on the other. In one section he lists 298 "elements of culture" common to Bible lands and Middle America in prehistoric times, ranging literally from "A" (adobe bricks) to "Z" (zodiacal sequence).

The New World Archeological Foundation, organized a few years ago by Mormons and financed largely with Mormon contributions, has for several years been carrying on exploration and excavations in southern Mexico among ruins of the prehistoric epochs during which they believe the Sumerian and Israelite colonies were founded in the Americas. While quite willing to explain their beliefs when the occasion seems appropriate, the Latter-day Saints for the most part avoid the heated, bitter debates that have characterized this general area of subject matter, although they resent the fact that gentile anthropologists will not take *The Book of Mormon* seriously enough even to become familiar with its contents or give it a fair trial as an authentic historical source. Mormons are confident that archeology will fully substantiate their beliefs about the prehistoric inhabitants of America, just as it has confirmed many of the cities and events described in the Bible. I taught one summer in Utah, where perhaps half of my students at the state university were Mormon. Outside class, the question of American Indian origins never came up at all, and even in class the students showed a more relaxed attitude toward moot questions than I had anticipated, for the very day I arrived in Salt Lake City the newspaper carried a warning from one of the church officials to a statewide youth meeting that the Devil was known to try to poison students' minds through the plausible-sounding teachings of university professors. (I heard Billy Sunday tell a tabernacle full of South Carolina college students and faculty the same thing about forty years ago.) The next most aggressive Mormon statement I have encountered was an extremely mild one in a 1924 book by Lewis Edward Hills, *New Light on American Archaeology.* Quoting the Eighty-second Psalm, "They have taken crafty counsel against God's hidden ones," Hills explained that the ancient Americans were God's hidden ones, and the counsel and craftiness were subsequent attempts to destroy the belief that these people were Israelites. "This," Hills added, "I believe, is still going on."

According to Hills, the Land of Many Waters, Rivers and Fountains (Mormon 701:5) was the Valley of Mexico; the Tower of Sherrizah was the Pyramid of the Sun at Teotihuacan, which many U.S. tourists have visited; Behor was what is now the ruined Cholula, and Ammonihah (Mormon 360: 14, 15) was Tikal, the greatest Maya ruin known, buried deep in the Petén jungle of northern Guatemala and now being explored by the University Museum in Philadelphia. The City Bountiful of *The Book of Mormon* (545:25, 26) was in the northern part of the land, Bountiful, in foothills overlooking lagoons near the Gulf of Mexico. The Church of Jesus Christ of Latter-day Saints believes in present-day and continuous revelation, says the *Encyclopaedia Britannica,* "by direct word of mouth and visible presence of God; by voice communication without visible presence; by visitation of angels and deliverance of messages; also by impressions upon the mind of men by the Spirit of God. Revelation in any of these manners is the supreme source of knowledge, and the final arbiter of doctrine for the Church, even superior to the written word." Lewis Hills experienced the second of these types of revelation as he was trying to locate on a map of Mexico the hill named Shim mentioned in *The Book of Mormon.* "I started to mark it on the map north of the city of Desolation. As I started to put it down a voice spoke to me and said, 'The hill on the other side.' I looked immediately at my Rand & McNally map before me, and there, sure enough, I saw a mountain called 'Mount Zem.' *The Book of Mormon* called it the hill Shim, and it is called Mount Zem. It is very clear to me: Shim and Zem are the same."

5

DR. PHUDDY DUDDY
AND THE
CRACKPOTS

THE STRAINED RELATIONS which fairly generally obtain between the professionals on the one hand and the thousands of Lost Continent, Lost Tribes, and Egyptian enthusiasts on the other, stem, as we have seen, from four centuries of controversy over the origin of the American Indians, especially the Maya and Aztecs of Mexico and Central America and the Inca and other great Andean civilizations of South America. Because they are of nearly unanimous consensus on an Asia-to-Alaska version of the peopling of the New World—some are also willing to admit sporadic and much later contacts across the Pacific from southeast Asia—the professional anthropologists are looked on by supporters of the other theories as mentally fossilized ivory-tower isolationists, while the Ph.D.'s regard their amateur harriers as, at best, misguided mystics whose theorizing in such scholarly fields is emotional rather than intellectual.

The mystics by no means deny this aspect of their doctrines.

The late Ralph M. Lewis, revered leader of the Rosicrucian Order, wrote in an article called "Science and Mysticism" in 1950: "The experiences of mysticism seem to originate entirely *within* the being of the individual. Further, they bring a gratification to him which goes far beyond the physical and intellectual pleasures." Advocates of what the professionals rather crossly speak of as "the wild theories" are drawn to their subject as irresistibly as an addict to his drug; they are willing and anxious to settle down to discuss it all afternoon with anyone showing the faintest interest. Since they are therefore somewhat brusquely avoided by almost any intended professional audience, the amateurs tend to picture themselves as intellectually persecuted or at least snubbed martyrs.

For example, Thor Heyerdahl, whose best-selling *Kon-Tiki* and *Aku-Aku,* as we shall see in a later chapter, gave his Peru-to-Oceania theory of American Indian cultural relationships a following fast approaching in size that of the Israelite and Atlantis schemes, wrote bitterly of the hardheaded opposition he encountered "in a dark office on one of the upper floors of a big museum in New York." Most readers are probably right in identifying Heyerdahl's villain as the Museum of Natural History. "The old man" he talked to there was "white-haired and good-humored," a description that is hard to pin on any one person at a museum, but according to the author this scientist's typical comments on Heyerdahl's theories were "No!" "Never!" "You're wrong, absolutely wrong. . . ." This violent reaction to Heyerdahl's remarkable hypothesis can, after all, be goaded from almost any professional anthropologist right now, but then the adventurer has his venerable foil, who had written books that "hardly ten men had read," deliver himself of the astonishing opinion that "the task of science is investigation pure and simple . . . not to try to prove this or that." A good many years ago this could have been the late Franz Boas, anthropologist at Columbia University, who often said that we need to collect more data before venturing too far afield into theory, but Boas died long before Heyerdahl got the

Flood myth pictured in an ancient Maya book, the Codex Dresden. Lost Tribes enthusiasts believe this was the American Indian version of the Old Testament story.

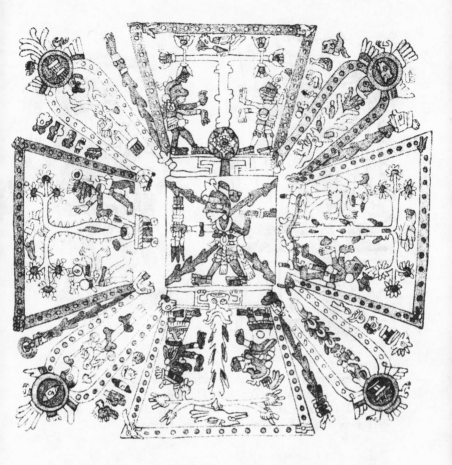

Upper left: Carved stone disk from southeastern Mexico showing a bearded figure with Semitic-like profile. Mormons contend that this is an Israelite. *After P. Keleman.*

Lower left: Mexican god, Quetzalcoatl, whom the Mormons identify with Christ, depicted in the Codex Magliabecchiano.

Above: Stylized trees in the Mexican Codex Fejérváry. Early Spanish priests thought these represented Christ's cross; the Mormons believe they depict the Tree of Life and events in *The Book of Mormon.*

The Mexican Morning Star Sacrifice as depicted in the ancient Mexican Codex Nuttal (Zouche). The Mormons identify the Mexican god, Quetzalcoatl, with Christ and consider the Morning Star ceremony a New World version of the crucifixion.

chilly treatment in New York and few or any of his followers share his extreme caution.

T. S. Denisen, a printer by profession and a philologist by avocation, who after years of painstaking study decided that the Mexican Indian languages were of Indo-European extraction, complained in the preface of his 1913 opus, "I received no *aid* whatever. Though I sought advice from philologists, it was for various reasons declined. One learned 'linguist,' however, discussing some preliminary work, took some pains to show that I must be a very ignorant person. His extraordinary conclusion was that 'not a single one' of my derivations would stand the test of scientific analysis, which was a little worse than I could say of his criticisms, since *some* of them happened to be just. Another philologist speaking in a semi-official capacity took a shorter cut, he flatly condemned *without reading my paper!*" Probably no franker self-appraisal ever unwittingly appeared in a book.

Harold S. Gladwin, a well-to-do amateur anthropologist, who financed his own excavations, maintained a museum in Arizona, and published his own volumes of what most professionals considered outrageous theories, often pictured himself in his popular book, *Men Out of Asia*, as a crusader trying to bludgeon some common sense into the stupid Ph.D.'s. "All the lights in the House of the High Priests of American Anthropology are out," he wrote, "all the doors and windows are shut and securely fastened (they do not sleep with their windows open for fear that a new idea might fly in); we have rung the bell of Reason, we have banged on the door with Logic, we have thrown the gravel of Evidence against their windows; but the only sign of life in the house is an occasional snore of Dogma."

Gladwin was well acquainted with most of the leading American anthropologists of his generation but delighted in badgering them in his book, which was illustrated with such telling caricatures that they left little doubt among the professionals and graduate students which eggheads he chose to lampoon.

Dr. Phuddy Duddy and his captive audience, a strait-jacketed
student. From Harold S. Gladwin's *Men Out of Asia*.

A true note of bitterness, though, crept into his usually light-hearted onslaughts against the academic world. "If you have ever visited a museum of archaeology and talked to the curator, or if you have ever taken a course in any branch of anthropology at any of our universities," he generalized recklessly, "you will undoubtedly experience the feeling that you have met Dr. Duddy somewhere, sometime. [Dr. Phuddy Duddy—for Ph.D.—was Gladwin's foil in *Men Out of Asia*.] You have—since our Phuddy Duddy is nothing less than a composite of all the great minds which have governed our anthropological thinking during the last 70 years." Dr. Duddy is always pompous: "This trespassing by amateurs in specialized fields," Gladwin has him trumpet at one point, "is a practice which cannot be too strongly condemned, and one which, unless quickly checked, will almost certainly stimulate unwarranted speculations. . . ."

This was more than mere professional and good-natured chiding; it recalls the attitude which prompted Augustus Le Plongeon, the engineer, practicing lawyer, self-styled doctor of medicine, and independent archeologist, to write, almost fifty years earlier:

But who are these *pretended authorities?* Certainly not the doctors and professors at the head of the universities and colleges in the United States; for not only do they know absolutely nothing of ancient American civilization, but judging from letters in my possession, the majority of them refuse to learn anything concerning it. . . . The so-called learned men of our days are the first to oppose new ideas and the bearers of these. This opposition will continue to exist until the arrogance of self-conceit of superficial learning that still hover within the walls of colleges and universities have completely vanished. . . .

So far as one can tell, Le Plongeon himself opposed no new idea whatsoever, on any grounds; as we have seen, he was an enthusiastic advocate of the Lost Continent of Atlantis, the Lost Tribes of Israel in America, theories that derived Egyptian civilization from the Maya of Yucatan and that sent north

African, Greek, and Chinese colonists to the Western Hemisphere in pre-Columbian times.

Even the mild-mannered Mormons, whose official Church dogma is the only one in which the American Indian figures, complain somewhat bitterly that *The Book of Mormon* has been unjustly disregarded as an authentic history of aboriginal civilizations in ancient America, and that this is deliberate stubbornness on the part of scientists. "However, strange as it may seem," wrote the Mormons Milton R. Hunter and Thomas S. Ferguson in 1950, "one hundred twenty years have passed since *The Book of Mormon* came from the press, and it has been almost completely ignored by those who should be interested in its claims because they profess to be seekers after truth. Reference is hereby being made to the archaeologists and anthropologists, students of American antiquities."

A. Hyatt Verrill, who believes that man came to America in various ways, some from Europe via Greenland, others across the Atlantic, some from Lost Atlantis or southern Europe, some by Bering Strait, and still others across the Pacific, pictures a deliberate plot on the part of professional archeologists to suppress information that conflicts with their theories. In a 1953 book co-authored with his wife, he depicts the scientists as now reluctantly forced to admit evidence that they had hidden for a long time, for example the existence of wheeled toys in prehistoric Mexico. The ancient Indians' lack of wheeled vehicles and, as was once thought, the fact that they never invented the wheel at all, have long been cited as evidence against any historical connection between the Old World and prehistoric America. "The archaeologists of Mexico had long known that the ancient Mexicans knew and used the wheel," the Verrills charged, "and there were numerous specimens of wheeled toys, etc., in the Museo Nacional, but for some unknown and mysterious reason, perhaps merely to sustain their denial of any Old World contacts, no North American scientist would publicly and openly admit the existence of the wheel in pre-Columbian times." "However," they added, in certain scientific papers never seen or read by the layman, there were, from time to time, brief references to wheels having been known to the early Americans. . . . Once the truth had been revealed it was useless to continue to maintain that wheels were unknown in ancient America and in *Natural History* . . . there was an article in which it was admitted. . . . Having finally openly admitted that the ancient Americans did know the wheel, the consciences of the 'die hards' were salved by stating that even if the early Americans did know the wheel, they made no practical use of it; which was all guesswork. . . . Once these anti–Old World–contacts archaeologists had been forced to admit the presence of the wheel in ancient America they began to see the light and to change their opinions in many ways.

There is something vastly amusing to professionals in this implied picture of anthropologists surreptitiously passing secret papers to fellow conspirators in order to guard the Fearful Truth of Wheeled Toys from a brain-washed public.

Harold S. Gladwin did not think it funny, though. He, too, felt that there was dirty work afoot. First he told how this absence of the wheel had been dinned into his unwilling ears, in season and out.

And then we learned that prehistoric wheels in Mexico had been discovered as far back as 1887, and, all the time we were being bullied, the Professors knew about them but decided the evidence could be ignored as the reference was obscure and had never been quoted. There's Science for you, with a big S.

In 1887, a Frenchman, Desiré de Charnay, was digging in southern Mexico and found several little clay animals with semicircular protuberances instead of legs, with a hole through each lump, making a sort of bearing. Four perforated clay disks accompanied each animal, and when Charnay pushed twigs through the disks and bearings, he had little wheeled toys that could be rolled back and forth on a board. This was all published in 1887 in his *Ancient Cities of the New World,* a book that is rarely mentioned and is rather scarce, probably due to most of the copies been brought up and burned by Dr. Phuddy Duddy.

Then in 1940, Matthew Stirling, Chief of the Bureau of American

Ethnology, digging at Tres Zapotes in Vera Cruz on the east coast of Mexico, found two more wheeled pottery toys, but in this case the axles ran through clay cylinders on which the little pottery dogs (?) were standing. It was only when we saw these toys illustrated in the *National Geographic* for September, 1940, that we learned the whole truth and came to realize the dastardly deception which had been practiced upon us.

There was one difference between this version and the Verrills' just quoted. Gladwin wrote in what *could* be called a jovial style, if it became necessary to do so. But non-existent deception has never been the subject of humor for its own sake; Gladwin knew that for all its joviality, the point was unmistakable and would sink in.

The Verrills' wishful thinking along such lines is even more apparent in later passages, where they imagine that Mrs. Verrill's manuscript, *Gods Who Were Men*, revolutionized the thinking of the scientific world. They quote a letter from the Museum of Natural History's Dr. Junius Bird which purportedly shows his "change of heart" but which is actually a very cautiously worded attempt at courteously acknowledging receipt of a manuscript for which he obviously had no enthusiasm. "Both Gordon Ekholm and I have read your book with considerable interest and appreciation at the time and effort you have put into it," goes the quotation. "Frankly, neither of us is qualified to evaluate much of your comparative material for it falls outside our experience and is from fields in which we have no training. . . . Many of your comparisons are significant. . . . Is it your intention that we should keep the volume on file here? If so, it will be available to anyone you may send in to see it." The deletions above are by the Verrills. They showed the letter to Dr. Rubin de la Borbolla, a Mexican anthropologist. "This is wonderful!" they quote him as saying.

In another passage the Verrills, in their name-dropping, tell that the late archeologist of Yale, Dr. Wendell C. Bennett, stated in a preliminary report on excavations at Tiahuanaco in South America that he found a stone wheel or grindstone.

"Later, however, when his report was published, all reference to the wheel was omitted." The inference is clear that he had deliberately suppressed the information. Again, near the end of their book the self-congratulating couple says of Mrs. Verrill's manuscript, she "confidently expected that the work would be discredited, derided and cast aside. But to her intense satisfaction and astonishment several leading archaeologists and scientists accepted her findings. One copy of the volume was presented to Dr. Earnest A. Hooton who placed the work in the Peabody Museum reference library. . . ." By 1953 Dr. Hooton was not alive to clarify this point, which unmistakably is intended to give the idea that in accepting the book for the Harvard library he was endorsing the Verrill views. Professional scholars for the most part are simply not used to playing this sort of ball. They do not quote one another's personal letters in their books, or cite verbal opinions without at least checking with the speaker.

Leo Wiener, a professor of Slavic at Harvard, who privately published an enormous and richly illustrated tome intended to prove that Maya and Aztec languages and culture were both derived from African Mandingo, wrote in his foreword: "Unquestionably, the archaeological dogs will continue to bay at the moon and will pursue the same vociferous methods as in the past, in order to suppress the search for the truth with noise where reason fails, forgetful that the truth, wherever it be, will shine forth without such vocal emphasis." Mr. Wiener had obviously had disheartening relations with American archeologists. He wrote of "the vile private and public aspersions" directed at himself; he stated that the Americanists were blinded by preconception; he ridiculed their cat-chasing-its-tail method, their Alice-in-Wonderland logic, and in one place he commented thus on the Brooklyn Museum's Dr. Herbert J. Spinden and his speculations regarding the subject content of inscriptions on a famous sixth-century Maya altar: "How Alice would have enjoyed this fantastic story, especially if Lewis Carroll had added: 'Maybe it represents the Follies of 503 or the follies of 1924.' "

Nor could the Le Plongeons ever believe that the professional anthropologists who rejected their wild theories were motivated by intellectual honesty. Le Plongeon ranted in print as sulphurically as his publishers would allow, and complained to friends that too much of his copy had been censored. Mme Le Plongeon, the former Miss Dixon of Brooklyn, was apparently a gentle soul, interested in music and poetry, and fiercely loyal to her much older and more cantankerous husband. When they returned to the United States in the 1880's from their years of field work in Yucatan, they settled in an old granite and brick mansion on Washington Street, Brooklyn; according to Willis Fletcher Johnson, who wrote a tribute to them in *The Outlook* forty years later, this home adjoined the original buildings of the Brooklyn Institute, both structures later demolished to make room for the railway approach to the Brooklyn Bridge. Here they kept huge stores of Maya relics and records, and waited in vain for the professional recognition that never came. According to Johnson they were bitterly disappointed.

Ears were deaf, eyes were blind, and doors were barred against them. A few, a very few, American scholars recognized the epochal value of their work and gave them credit for it. The majority were coldly indifferent or openly hostile. All the actors in the wretched tragedy are now dead, and I shall not recall their names. But some of the most influential leaders and patrons of American archaeological and ethnological research apparently set themselves to discredit Dr. Le Plongeon and to prevent recognition of his achievements. They derided him and denounced him as a romancer and fabricator, at par with the author of the notorious Cardiff Giant, then still fresh in memory. . . . So Dr. and Mrs. Le Plongeon got no adequate public hearing, and their books had to be published at their own expense. Yet to-day all the revelations which they then made and which were ridiculed and rejected are completely verified.

Professional anthropologists have scarcely ever felt it necessary to reply to these charges, for they let Le Plongeon's absurdities speak for themselves: his conviction that certain creases on Maya monuments indicated they had the electrical telegraph in prehistoric times, that Jesus spoke pure Maya on the cross, that the shape of a reclining statue, the Chac Mool of Yucatan, symbolized the outline of North and South America, thus proving that the ancient Indians were intimately familiar with the entire hemisphere's geography. Le Plongeon was not only untrained and wholly inexperienced in analyzing and interpreting anthropological data, but he was also completely uncritical of his own methods, possibly one more expression of the egotism so unabashedly displayed in his account of real or fancied experiences. After Le Plongeon thought that he had convinced the Indians that he was a reincarnated Maya god, according to Johnson they revealed to him "much of the ancient lore of the Mayas which was withheld from the common people, including the meaning of many of the hieroglyphs and many of the proper names and other words of the ancient Maya language. They also told him in detail the story of the tragic downfall of the Maya Empire and the relationship of Maya civilization and mythology to that of Egypt and India."

All of these are bald falsehoods, either by Johnson or by Le Plongeon. No Maya Indian in 1886 had any notion of ancient Maya history, civilization, or mythology, and even today few if any of them have ever heard of Egypt and India. Furthermore this passage illustrates another favorite deceit of Le Plongeon's. He always claimed that he could "read" the Maya hieroglyphic inscriptions. What he actually meant was that, like anyone else, he could give his own personal interpretation of scenes depicted on sculpture, murals, and in the codices. But he never said this explicitly, and to the non-expert his words meant that he could read the ancient writing as one might read Egyptian phonetic hieroglyphs, or Greek, or English. As for the meaning of proper names and other Maya words "withheld from the common people," these are not now and never have been secret; they were available to anyone who asked or listened, as numerous Maya dictionaries from the sixteenth century onward will attest.

The antagonism between the professionals and amateurs extends also to the professionals and the true mystics. A member of the Rosicrucian Order, writing on "When Was America Settled?" in the *Rosicrucian Digest* in 1954, noted that books on the Lost Continents had been dismissed "with condescending amusement," and that occult science, "which alone could interpret Indian traditions of migration and settlement, was regarded as a queer vagary of a few fanatical pundits." He complained that when occultists sought funds for expeditions and research, they "were brushed aside as eccentrics incapable of making honest and unbiased inquiries." Another Rosicrucian, Walter J. Albersheim, Sc.D., writing on science and mysticism in 1953, asked, "Why the bitterness and scorn, the personal hatred that many scientists and would-be scientists heap on everyone who dares defend mystical endeavor . . . ?" Albersheim thought that the cause of this "unwillingness to see or listen, this personal vilification" was insecurity, and that it revealed itself in the very bitterness of the hatred itself. But the same question occurred to him that occurs to me: "Is there anything in mysticism that can arouse suspicion and fear in scientists?"

The late Mme H. P. Blavatsky, the most revered of the mystic Theosophists, wrote in her famous *Secret Doctrine*, "It is the ignorance of our men of science who will accept neither the tradition that several Continents have already sunk, nor the periodical law which acts throughout the Manvantaric Cycle—it is this ignorance that is the chief cause of all the confusion." Elsewhere she again expressed her scorn of the orthodox scientist: quoting a Theosophist on his beliefs regarding Peruvian antiquities, she commented that he was a "rara avis among scientific men, a fearless searcher, who accepts the truth wherever he finds it, and is not afraid to speak it out in the very face of dogmatic opposition. . . ."

Along with this defiance of professional criticism, the amateurs and mystics often manifest a paradoxical modesty, even hesitance, in presenting their beliefs to the public. They are typically pessimistic. Perhaps Albersheim's hypothesis on insecurity might be considered for his fellow travelers instead. The most widely read champion of the Atlantis theory, Lewis Spence, was prepared for the worst in 1925: "Doubtless prejudices and prepossessions will beset my way, and the value of my premises will be denied by those of clearer vision, just as others may, by virtue of a higher gift of dialectic, succeed in overturning my general thesis. . . ." T. S. Denisen, an amateur philologist, prophesied: "I shall undoubtedly be accused of rashness in suggesting daring derivation where greater scholars have been cautious. . . . Where others have held back I have boldly entered, not from temerity and presumption but from necessity. He who would sail unchartered waters must take chances."

Samuel G. Drake, too, writing about 1840, anticipated ridicule from critics: "Before we had known, that, if we were in error, it was in the company of philosophers, such as we have in this chapter introduced to our readers, we felt a hesitancy in avowing our opinions upon a matter of so great moment. But, after all, as it is only matter of honest opinion, no one should be intolerant, although he may be allowed to make himself and even his friends merry at our expense." And Mrs. Hyatt Verrill, a little over a century later, "confidently expected that her work would be discredited, derided, and cast aside."

One cannot help but see some regularity in these attitudes. The typical advocate of the "wild" theories of American Indian origins begins his book with the underdog appeal; he points out that he has been personally scorned, ridiculed, or at best snubbed by the professionals. Then he predicts that his writings will in turn be ill received or ignored, and he proceeds to attack the thickheaded bigotry of the men in universities and museums. Frequently he implies that they are not only hopelessly conservative and jealous of any scholarly inroads by amateurs but also that they are actually dishonest, and when confronted with conflicting evidence they will suppress or if necessary destroy it. Still, though blasting the professionals as ignorant, incompetent, and unethical, the pseudo-scientists almost invariably take pride in any real or (more often) fancied approval they obtain from these misguided Phuddy Duddies. The Verrills boasted shamelessly of professional comments which they mistakenly interpreted as favorable to their writings; and of all people in the world, whom did Gladwin ask to write the preface and thus lend some prestige to his book which had devoted its every page to ridiculing the university professor and museum curator? None other than Ph.D. Earnest Albert Hooton, professor of anthropology and curator of physical anthropology in the Peabody Museum of Harvard University!

Another sort of paradoxical behavior on the part of the mystics is their proud avowal on the one hand that they are not bound by the scientists' rules of empirical research and are quite willing to use intuition or supernaturally derived evidence in their "research," at the same time continually protesting that they are as scientific as anyone else in their methods.

The amateurs will always hate the Phuddy Duddies, and the professionals will forever scorn the Crackpots.

6

MEN OUT OF ASIA

THE AMERICAN INDIAN origin theory held
today by most of the professional anthropologists whom Le
Plongeon, Gladwin, Heyerdahl, and the Rosicrucians and Theosophists have written about so indignantly, seems not at all
unreasonable to its advocates. From time to time during geological history, the narrow stretch of what is nowadays water
between the pinched northeastern end of the Eurasian continent and the westernmost point of Alaska has been either a
land bridge or a frozen strip that animals of most kinds could
cross safely. Between the great glaciations, this region around
Bering Strait was much warmer than it is today, probably covered, according to Richard Foster Flint's *Glacial and Pleistocene Geology,* with long thick grass, ideal fodder for elephants
and other herbivores. Over it at one time or another have
trooped bears, mammoths, reindeer, bison, camels, and
other animals. This traffic, says Flint, has been mostly east-
bound, but some, including that of camels, was westbound, and
during the Pleistocene epoch was limited to animals of cold-
temperate or boreal habitat.

Even a primitive Old Stone Age man, once he mastered the

north Siberian environment sufficiently to wander as far as the Kamchatka Peninsula, could surely have crossed and, according to anthropologists, surely did, in evidence of which they point to the continuous geographical distribution of a long list of functionally or historically linked archeological artifacts and later objects and customs which extend across northern Europe and Asia and over into America—such things as the sinew-backed bow, slat armor, snowshoes, the toboggan, bark boats, bark dishes and pots, basketry hats, the teepee or conical tent of skin and bark, divination by examining the shoulderblade, ceremonies centered around the bear, the "magic flight" story, and specific pottery types like cord-marked pottery which extended deep into the southeastern United States in prehistoric times.

In view of what anthropologists consider a demonstrable flow of culture from Asia to America via Bering Strait, which even today is only about fifty miles across, with several island hops to break the stretches of open sea—you can see across it on most days—and in view of the great diversity of American Indian physical types or sub-races that either have been excavated in skeletal form or survive as remnants among current aboriginal populations, the most widely accepted anthropological theory is that America was peopled over a long period, beginning at least twenty-five thousand and perhaps more years ago, in successive waves by many different groups of wandering hunters, different branches of basically Mongoloid Asiatic populations.[1] Although rapid migration was doubtless possible, this expansion probably took place slowly, for nomadic or semi-nomadic hunters typically move from their familiar ground only when forced to do so by scarcity or migration of

[1] There is still a wide range of informed opinion on the time of man's arrival in America. Dr. George F. Carter, a geographer, contends that man reached the San Diego area of California as early as 100,000 years ago. Dr. James B. Griffin, an archeologist, although granting that a number of discoveries support the argument that man may have been in the New World some 20,000 to 30,000 years ago, does not feel that as yet any of them clearly demonstrates that this was so earlier than 10,000 to 12,000 B.C.

the game on which they subsist, or by the pressure of other groups behind them, or by the economic necessity for growing populations of this type to divide, with seceding groups seeking new hunting grounds. Changing climate or other habitat conditions may also bring about movement, but these usually take place so slowly as to be almost indiscernible over the centuries.

John Josselyn traveled extensively in New England beginning in 1638, and about thirty-four years later published two works, *New England Rarities* (1672) and (in 1673) an account of his two voyages to the New World. In the former he stated: "The north-east people of America, that is, N. England, &c., are judged to be Tartars, called Samoades, being alike in complexion, shape, habit and manners." In the second work he wrote: "The Mohawks are about 500; their speech a dialect of the Tartars (as also is the Turkish tongue)." Cotton Mather, not much later in the same century, declared in his *Magnalia Christi Americana* that Julius Caesar, when he said of the fierce, nomadic, Black Sea Scythians that it "is harder to find them than to foil them," was actually referring also to the American Indians. Pierre de Charlevoix, who visited North America in 1720, quoted Solinus and Pliny, as well as the Venetian Marco Polo, to the effect that the Scythians engaged in vast migrations, abandoning great regions and moving into uninhabited countries, probably at one stage reaching America itself.

The Bering Strait theory evidently goes back even farther than Josselyn's works, for it was under attack at least as early as 1637, when Thomas Morton, in his natural history of New England, protested that the motivations for crossing what he supposed was then a frozen land with nothing solid in sight ahead were not sufficient. Today Lost Continent advocates ask what is so different between their theories and this professional anthropological view, for both propose the submergence below the ocean of a land mass, occupied by human beings in one case, traversed by them in another. They wonder why the professionals so unanimously reject sunken continents but are quite willing to hypothesize a former land bridge from Siberia to Alaska. For answers the anthropologists refer you to their geological colleagues, and the oceanographers, who have mapped almost every foot of the sea's floor between these northernmost corners of the hemispheres, can tell you almost exactly what the terrain was like when it was above water, and will hazard reasoned guesses on the geological period and number of years ago that the submergences took place. The only question seems to be whether the land bridge was caused by a lowered sea level or by crustal warping, the actual movement of the earth's surface as its relatively weak substratum gave way under the enormous weight of a large ice sheet and then adjusted upward when the glacier receded.

The land bridge at Bering Isthmus was wide, a gently rolling land with lakes of considerable size, and a number of small rivers. The Yukon, for example, emptied into the lower sea by one of these old channels now about thirty fathoms below the ocean. When this land was exposed, it held back the Arctic Ocean and thus allowed the warmer Pacific currents to temper the climate of the southern side of the isthmus. With sea level thirty fathoms lower than it is now, the Arctic Ocean would lie more than three hundred miles north of Bering Strait. From his study of undersea charts Dr. Douglas S. Byers of the Robert S. Peabody Foundation at Andover, Massachusetts, tells us that what is now the shortest approach, between Cape Deshneva and Cape Prince of Wales, separated by only twenty nautical miles of open water, was not the most ancient route for pedestrian traffic, but that instead a route from Cape Chaplina north of St. Lawrence Isle toward Norton Sound, now crossing about one hundred and ten miles of open sea, was the most favorable land passage for the Stone Age invaders of the Americas. But if questioned about former land masses in the Atlantic or Pacific oceans, geologists and oceanographers become much vaguer in their details and begin to talk in terms of millions, not thousands, of years ago, long before Man appeared on earth.

Professional anthropologists also believe that for the most part the higher civilizations of the Americas—the Maya, pre-Aztec Mexican, Pueblo, and pre-Inca Andean—developed independently of Old World influences, and indeed to a great extent independently of each other. Here the non-professionals hold their heads in anguished disapproval and point to similar or even identical objects, customs, legends, and religious beliefs or practices found in both the Old and New Worlds; they feel that these things speak for themselves, and they look on the professionals' technically worded explanations in terms of "parallel inventions in response to configurations of similar stimuli" as a jargon-camouflaged weaseling out of a tough spot.

Hundreds of thousands of words, earnest, impassioned, and often irate, have flowed in this classical debate. From the huge corpus of evidence cited by the professionals in defense of their position, here is a sample: agriculture. High civilization, like the cultures of ancient Egypt, Mesopotamia, Persia, and the Indus Valley, cannot develop without some effective food production, in most cases cultivation of food crops, usually storable cereals that can be kept in surplus quantities, thus making possible leisure time and non-farmer specialists for other activities. This was true also of the ancient American high cultures, but the inventory of crops here was quite different from that of pre-Columbian Asia, Africa, or Europe. There were, for example, in the New World no rice, wheat, millet, barley, flax, rye, oats, nor any of the Old World cultivation techniques—no plow, no domesticated oxen to draw it, no wheeled vehicles even, nor any of the tamed animals so closely associated with agricultural civilizations abroad: no horses, pigs, sheep, chickens, water buffalo or livestock of any kind.

Only the dog was common to both hemispheres, and a few domesticated plants: sweet potatoes, gourds, cotton, and coconuts. In America were none of the Old World's fruit trees—

such as apple, peach, pear, banana—and in the Eastern Hemisphere no American turkeys, Peruvian llamas or alpacas, or Indian tobacco, although most of these will thrive when transplanted to the other continents. We forget these old distributions today when Turkish tobacco is as well known as Central American bananas, Georgia peaches, and Washington apples. Dr. Alfred L. Kroeber adds the following Old World elements that had not made their way into the Americas by 1492: proverbs, divination by examination of viscera, iron, the wheel—except by independent invention here as a toy and for ritual figures—stringed musical instruments except the monotone bow, oaths, and ordeals. He thinks that the following were independently invented in each hemisphere: the concept and use of zero in mathematics, the two-headed bird symbol (except the post-Columbian Hapsburg eagle brought to Mexico by Maximilian), the corbeled arch of overlapping stones (in contrast to the true arch with its self-supported keystone vault), the use of five supplementary days in the year's calendar, a zodiacal sequence, permutative time counts, addiction to gambling, intoxicants, fermentation started by saliva, half-hitch and single-rod coiling in basketry, and in textiles the use of looms and tie-dyeing, Pan's pipe pitches, bronze and other metallurgy. One can imagine the wordage required to debate each item in this imposing list.

There is also a long list of parallel cultural traits on either side of the Pacific about which there is still doubt of their independent invention or relatedness. An almost identical patolli-parcheesi game was played in both hemispheres, and in art, architecture, and religion, as well as in some material techniques, astonishing similarities lead many anthropologists to admit sporadic, possibly accidental Pacific crossings from southeast Asia, which may have brought over some isolated religious concepts, art motifs, or even objects. But most scholars do not feel that these were of lasting cultural or racial importance.

In 1827, John Ranking, in *Historical Researches on the*

Conquest of Peru, Mexico, etc., proposed that the Inca empire of South America was founded by the crews of a few of Kublai Khan's ships driven eastward across the Pacific after escaping the storm which wrecked the major part of the fleet the Mongol emperor sent against Japan in the thirteenth century. Hubert Howe Bancroft, who tended to criticize with devastating courtesy, wrote in 1886:

In this, as in all other theories, but little distinction is made between the introduction of foreign culture, and the actual origin of the people. It would be absurd, however, to suppose that a few ships' crews, almost, if not quite, without women, cast accidently ashore in Peru in the thirteenth century, should in the fifteenth be found to have increased to a mighty nation, possessed of a civilization quite advanced, yet resembling that of their mother country so slightly as to afford only the most faint and far-fetched analogies. . . . It is ridiculous to suppose that a Mongol father imparted to his children a knowledge of the arts and customs of Asia, without impressing upon their minds the story of his shipwreck and the history of his native country, about which all Mongols are so precise.

A somewhat similar hypothesis was advanced by Harold S. Gladwin in his *Men Out of Asia* in 1947. Gladwin suggested that after the death of Alexander the Great in 323 B.C., some survivors of his wrecked fleet under Admiral Nearchus sailed eastward, picking up artisans in India and southeastern Asia, and made an epic voyage across the Pacific, where they and their descendants were responsible for the pre-Columbian high civilizations of the Maya region and the Peruvian Andes. Reviewing this book for *American Antiquity*, Dr. Samuel Kirkland Lothrop admitted that the great triremes, quadriremes, and quinqueremes of Alexander's fleet, with crews of five and six hundred men, were indeed powerful enough to cross the Pacific, but not under sail in the tropics against prevailing winds and currents as shown on weather maps today. Moreover, they would have lacked the compass which made it possible for the later fifteenth- and sixteenth-century explorers to hold course without the aid of sun or stars, and "also made it possible to turn around and go home."

But granted for the sake of argument, continued Dr. Lothrop, that boatloads of assorted Asiatics reached South America with their technical skills, why did they leave no traces in the islands along the way; how did they develop both temperate and tropical agriculture in the New World; why did they give one tribe a back-scratcher, another a drinking tube, a third a house on stilts; why did they give the Peruvians a decimal system and the Maya a vigesimal system of numbers; and why are the languages in these areas unrelated? Most important of all, said Dr. Lothrop, Gladwin ignored the flourishing agricultural communities that existed without pottery or metal a thousand or more years before Nearchus.

In 1836, J. MacKintosh, who had so stoutly attacked the Israelite theory of American Indian origins, as enthusiastically insisted that they were derived from Korea. MacKintosh claimed that when the powerful Kitans defeated the Koreans during the Tsin dynasty, they so tyrannized their victims that the latter undertook a voyage to establish a colony in some distant land. For nine weeks they sailed northeast, through several islands, "and arrived in a country, whose bounds they could not discover. This land Santini, very reasonably, supposes to be America. This information . . . tends to prove beyond the possibility of a doubt, that the Coreans were the first that visited the new world from Asia."

Of all these Asiatic theories, the one that attracted the most attention in scientific congresses of the past century was that which identified a country called Fu-Sang in early Chinese annals with prehistoric Mexico. A Frenchman, De Guines, seems to have been, in 1761, the first to publish his opinion that in the fifth century of our era, some Buddhists were sent from China to establish their religion in the New World, which they called Fu-Sang. He apparently derived this hypothesis from a Chinese fable recorded by the seventh-century historian Li Yen, who, according to Channing Arnold and Frederick J.

Tabor Frost, had the tale from a Buddhist priest Hwui Shan, who said that he came from this unknown country 40,000 *li* east of China. Since a Chinese *li* is about one third of a mile, this would place Fu-Sang at least as far away as the Americas, but H. J. von Klaproth, who investigated the tale very thoroughly in 1831, attempted to demonstrate that Fu-Sang was actually the southeast coast of Japan, and that the 40,000-*li* distance, besides being in a very variable measure, could scarcely have been estimated accurately by a Buddhist priest, and besides it was probably on a par, according to another investigator, E. Morse, with the "mulberry trees thousands of feet high and the silkworms 7 feet long which form part of his fairy tale." Arnold and Frost point out further that glazed roofing tile, so common in China from 2000 B.C. onward, was entirely absent in ancient Central America, as were the potter's wheel and the plow.

In 1844 another Frenchman, a M. de Paravey, renewed the De Guines hypothesis, and a year later, Friederich de Neuman, professor of Oriental languages at the University of Munich— one source calls him Neumann de Monaco—also supported it. Baron von Humboldt also found zodiac signs in the Hindu lunar mansions that reminded him of the ancient Mexican calendar, and he concluded that Asiatic and Mexican astrology had a common origin. As early as 1866 the French architect, Viollet-le-Duc, noted striking resemblances between ancient Mexican structures and those of southern India. All these investigators were impressed with the similarity of the Brahma-Siva-Vishnu trinity on the one hand, and the Mexican Ho-Huitzilopochtli-Tlaloc trinity on the other, with resemblances in the attributes of certain Hindu deities and those of the Maya pantheon, and with likenesses between pagodas of India and the pyramidal temples of Meso-America. Extending their comparisons southward to Peru, they noted analogous gods like Pachacamac and Viracocha there, and the so-called Virgins of the Sun seemed to be counterparts of the female servants of the Far Eastern deities. Some enthusiasts, according to Rivero and Tschudi in 1853, regarded Fo in China, Buddha in Japan, Sommono-Cadom in India, Lamaism in Tibet, the doctrine of Dschakdschiamuni among the Mongols and the Calmuks, as well as the worship of Quetzalcoatl in Mexico and of Mango-Capac in Peru as but so many branches of the same trunk. Rivero and Tschudi themselves urged that Quetzalcoatl and Mango-Capac were both missionaries of Brahma or Buddha worship, and probably of different sects.

From then on to the end of the century, a long series of scholars, most of them French, supported all or some part of the general idea that native American civilization derived from or was at least influenced by Chinese or Asiatic-Buddhist culture. In 1874 Lucien Adam said that Matthew Fontaine Maury, the famous nineteenth-century geographer and Confederate naval commander, had assured him that Chinese mariners would have had no serious difficulty in discovering America. One could go from China via Japan, the Kuriles, the Kamchatka coast, and the Aleutians to Alaska without losing sight of land for more than a few hours.

Again we must not leave a theory of this type without reference to Augustus Le Plongeon, whom we have quoted so often, for the good doctor put his oar into the waters of just about every possible hypothesis that he or anyone else could create about prehistoric America: Atlantis, the Lost Tribes, Queen Moo and the Egyptians, the Phoenicians, and the Greeks in the New World. It is scarcely to be expected that he would decline this distinction to the Chinese. Describing some Peruvian figures that seemed Chinese to him, he showed them to "a learned Chinaman." According to Le Plongeon, the Chinaman's features portrayed vividly the different emotions that preyed upon his mind: "curiosity, surprise, awe, superstitious fear. . . . After much ado and coaxing, he at last told me, in a voice full of reverence as a Brahmin would in uttering the sacred word O-A-UM, that the meaning of the inscription was Fo." Apparently it did not occur to Le Plongeon that the giant's monologue in *Jack and the Beanstalk* might be even closer approximation of these fearsome words.

The most searching examination of pre-Columbian trans-Pacific contacts is that of two English authors of *The American Egypt*, Channing Arnold and Frederick J. Tabor Frost, and of two modern anthropologists, Dr. Gordon F. Ekholm and Dr. Robert Heine-Geldern of the Museum of Natural History. In several individual and collaborated publications these scholars have assembled an astounding number of parallels between the New World cultures and those of ancient India, China, and Mesopotamia. Dr. Ekholm suggests that Asiatic influences in Mexico may focus on the western border of the Maya area in the present states of Chiapas, Tabasco, or Campeche, and that they are found in greatest strength in the late Mexican-influenced motifs and styles of Chichen Itza, Yucatan, and the contemporaneous city of Tula in central Mexico, about A.D. 1200. This complex of Asiatic influences may have reached America by A.D. 700.

Dr. Ekholm does not maintain that any one of these cultural parallels between Asia and America is itself conclusive, but he does feel that some are important, and that taken together they all tend to reinforce one another, for they occur in contexts that are contemporary or otherwise related. The list of almost identical or very similar traits, discussed in great detail by Arnold and Frost in 1905 and later by Ekholm and Heine-Geldern, includes the "fire-serpent" and mythical sea-monster, atlantean figures, gods or ceremonial figures standing on crouched humans, stylized or celestial trees with demonic faces in their branches, stairways flanked by serpent balustrades, architectural half-columns, colonnettes, trefoil arches, vaulted galleries, sculptured panels depicting figures grouped around personages on low platform-thrones, specific postures of enthroned figures, tiger thrones, lotus thrones, lotus staffs, phallic cults, seated lions or tigers, sun discs, and diving gods.

As an outstanding example of how close the resemblances

between Asia and Meso-America can be, Ekholm and Heine-Geldern cite the Hindu-Buddhist and Maya lotus motifs. In both we find the unusual custom of featuring the root-like stalk or rhizome which in the real plant grows horizontally under water or deeply buried in mud, instead of the flowers or leaves themselves, which rise above the surface on their own stalks. In both, the lotus plant is often used as a "kind of imaginary landscape animated by human figures," the latter frequently

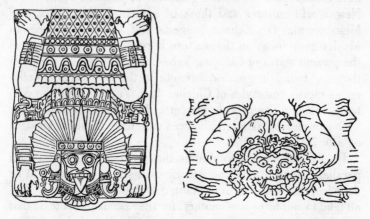

Diving gods. *Left:* Sculpture from Veracruz, Mexico. *After G. F. Ekholm, illustrated by J. Imbelloni. Right:* Balinese manuscript.

shown in a reclining position holding on to the rhizome. In India the rhizome emerges from the mouths of sea monsters with fish-like bodies at both ends of the lotus plant; in Yucatan stylized fish occupy these same positions. And in both, the lotus panels serve as borders to larger and more important portions of the relief sculptures.

Heine-Geldern and Ekholm do not believe that these correspondences could have been due to mere accidental contacts, such as might have resulted from ships driven across the Pacific by storms and ocean currents. They feel sure that some kind of two-way traffic between southeast Asia and America must have taken place by ships capable of carrying sailors and merchants, "neither of whom we could expect to have been accomplished architects and sculptors or experts in cosmological lore and similar fields." There is little doubt that ships and navigation were sufficiently advanced for oceanic crossings at that time. The authors cite several examples of second- to fourth-century ships capable of making the voyage. Around A.D. 400, a Chinese Buddhist returned from India, directly across the ocean from Ceylon to Java, in a ship carrying more than two hundred sailors and merchants, a much larger vessel than the ships of Columbus and the early Spanish explorers.

Arnold and Frost suggest the most likely itinerary that would have brought early Buddhists to America.

They followed the course of the current to America and would be thrown on the coast where it struck in its greatest force. The Pacific Counter Current turns off into two branches on nearing the coast at about 10 degrees north latitude, part going to the south and part north. If they took the southern branch they would come in contact with the Equatorial Current coming up from Peru, and inevitably be carried out to sea again. On the other hand, if they took the northern branch, they would be carried for some miles along the coast until about latitude 13 degrees, where the current runs in close, and there would be the most probable spot for them to land.

Arnold and Frost made some interesting suggestions about what could have dislodged Buddhist movements toward America. They point out that persecution of Buddhists during the fourth and fifth centuries ended in the latter being driven out of India, to Burma and China, where Buddhism was acknowledged as the third religion of the Empire as early as A.D. 65. From Burma and the Malay Peninsula, the religion spread into the Indian Archipelago; a temple at Boro Budor in Java was begun between A.D. 600 and 700. But again in Burma the Buddhists became involved in disturbances, possibly part of widespread racial or ethnic tensions in this entire region, and Arnold and Frost suggest that probably about the eighth century a band of Buddhists undertook a voyage in search of a new home. Possibly, say the authors, these were Khmers, or some Eastern people professing Buddhism.

The archeological work of Emilio Estrada, Betty J. Meggers, and Clifford Evans in Ecuador revealed strong evidence of much earlier contacts between South America and eastern Asia. The Valdivia excavations on the coast of Ecuador yielded pottery made by a shellfish-gathering people between 2000 and 3000 B.C. These ceramics share a number of distinctive features with pottery of the Middle to Late Jomon period of Japan, which dates to the same period in prehistory. There is no other linked group of similar ceramic traits elsewhere on the Pacific coast of the Americas, where one would expect these shellfish-gatherers to have left remains if they had migrated by land. Estrada and Meggers present another list of dramatic similarities between Ecuadorian archeological remains of the early Bahia and early Jama-Coaque culture, dating to the last two centuries before Christ, and antiquities of approximately the same epoch in Japan, India, southeast Asia, and the nearby islands of Melanesia. The list of parallel or closely similar cultural traits includes pottery house models with architectural features not typical of New World house types, neck rests, seated figurines, symmetrically graduated panpipes, pottery net weights, ear ornaments shaped like golf tees, coolie yokes for carrying burdens, and sea-going rafts with center boards.

Like Arnold and Frost, these authors note that the counter-equatorial current, running eastward just north of the equator, leads directly toward the northern coast of Ecuador, and, farther to the north, the Japanese current flows eastward to join the Mexican current moving down along the Pacific coast to Ecuador. In reply to charges that a small group of foreigners appearing on South American shores would be liquidated or absorbed by the local inhabitants, Estrada and Meggers remind us that a few years after European discovery, in the early sixteenth century, seventeen Negroes survived a shipwreck off

this same coast, intermarried with Indian women, gained political control of the whole province of Esmeraldas in a short
time, and, decades later, successfully resisted the Spanish conquest. Furthermore, the authors feel that the period around
200 B.C. was an ideal one for the introduction of new ideas
into a culture which had emerged from its simple, primitive
beginnings and had the potential for developing into a relatively advanced civilization.

Estrada and Meggers assure us that southeast Asiatic ocean-
going vessels were quite capable of making the Pacific voyage
even at this early date. By the third century, such ships were
capable of carrying six hundred men and one thousand metric
tons of cargo, and long before that, heavily provisioned vessels
were using the sea lanes to maintain economic and political
relations between India, China, and their colonies.

The various theories recorded in this chapter have been presented with deliberately unemotional restraint. This does not
mean that they are characteristically so regarded. On the contrary, every hypothesis, every claim, every shred of evidence
has been hotly debated from New York to Vienna to Copen-
hagen. The International Congress of Americanists, held almost every year since 1875, has provided perhaps the most
consistently dramatic scenes in these debates, for here the ad-
versaries from all parts of the world can voice their opinions
face to face. Let us look at the first congress as an example:

It was Monday, July 19, 1875, at one-thirty of a hot afternoon in Nancy, France. The occasion was gala; the sponsoring
institution, the Council of the Société Américaine de France,
had gone all out to present a colorful display. The Ducal
Palace, where the sessions were held, was decorated at one end
with massed American flags, their staffs joined behind a large
shield bearing the names of Leif Erikson, Jean Cousin de
Dieppe, Christopher Columbus, and Americus Vespucius. At
the entrance to the Salle des Cerfs, where the delegates were
in session, a double "trophée" of French flags was crowned

with two large tapestry panels from the pavilion of Charles the Rash, Duke of Bourgogne. In the halls beyond was a large exhibit of American antiquities and native Indian curios, plus some Guanche relics from the Canary Islands, brought by Dr. Chil y Naranjo, an ardent champion of the Lost Atlantis theory.

Inside, delegates from thirty nations, having finished that morning the inevitable French congress rituals of welcome, response, and other formalities, had settled down now to the real purpose for which they came—the exchange of scholarly information and ideas about aboriginal America. There was an air of expectancy everywhere; the delegates seemed to sense the historical importance of this first meeting. By the high windows overlooking the park stood Professor Henry, director of the Smithsonian Institution in Washington, and Mr. Robert C. Winthrop, president of the Historical Society of Boston, official delegates from the United States. They were exchanging pleasantries with Messrs. Paplonski and Luis de Zélinski, who, according to the program, represented "Russia and the Slav Countries." As one looked about the crowded hall, one saw Ogivia Yémon from Japan, M. Stéphane D'Aristarchi from Constantinople, distinguished professors from Norway, Denmark, Peru and a host of other dignified scholars in their frock coats and high stiff collars.

Their first session was on the subject "Relations de l'Amérique précolombienne avec l'Ancien-Monde," a topic loaded with dynamite, and the delegates were obviously looking forward with more than purely academic relish to the impending clash of intellects. The first lecture, a harmless one on the Icelandic discovery of America, was by now old hat in these circles; it was politely ignored. The second paper on the program, read by M. Paul Gaffarel, professor of the Faculty of Letters at Dijon, was called "Phoenicians in America." The delegates sat forward, expecting some fireworks, but things had not yet warmed up sufficiently, and although there was a bit of head-shaking here and there, even this controversial topic elicited no protest. Then came a paper submitted by M.

Foucaux, professor of the Collége de France, entitled "Buddhism in America." As it proceeded, half the learned audience beamed assent, the other half began to fidget restlessly, with obvious growing annoyance.

The paper ended with its writer's expressed hope that the question of Buddhist influences in prehistoric America would be seriously considered by the delegates, whose researches, he felt, surely would establish for certain the degree to which America owed Asia a large part of its ancient civilization. That was asking for a fight, and by now there were willing contestants. Immediately M. Léon de Rosny, president of the Société d'Ethnologie de Paris, requested the floor. M. Eduard Madier de Montjau, presiding, granted it. "Bering Strait has never been a serious obstacle for communication between the two continents," De Rosny proclaimed.

Every year favorable winds blow from Kamchatka to America and there are more winds which blow back again. The Eskimos consider it sport to make the voyage from one peninsula to the other, not only in isolated boats but in large fishing fleets. Wouldn't it have been possible some fine day for the voyage to be tried, not by a few miserable seal hunters, but by large bands of emigrants from the more civilized regions of east Asia, who would not have stopped, like the Eskimo, at the Alaskan peninsula, but would have penetrated to Mexico, perhaps to Peru, and, in bringing to these regions new ideas of government and religion, would have founded the great civilizations attributed to the Toltecs, the Aztecs, and the Incas? . . . We do not admit either the autochthonism nor the non-autochthonism of the American races, because it is a matter of science and we cannot affirm it without proof. It is the same with the autochthonism or non-autochthonism of American civilizations. What *proofs* can one bring in favor of the Asiatic origin of Mexican or Peruvian civilization?

M. de Rosny stopped and deliberately poured a glass of water, touched it to his lips somewhat distastefully, and continued. "Not only is the solution of that question nowhere near at hand," he continued, "but even to pose it is premature.

They have not yet succeeded in deciphering most of the monuments of indigenous American literature, and yet they want to compare this civilization with that of Asia! They are just beginning to spell, and already they want to draw conclusions!"

There was some laughter and scattered applause. M. le docteur Dally, president of the Société d'Anthropologie de Paris, obtained the floor. "These alleged analogies between the Old World and the New are naught but empty semblances. The solution of the question is that the American natives are not Hindus, nor Phoenicians, nor Chinese, nor Europeans: they are Americans."

The next speaker was the Reverend Father Petitot, a missionary, who declared this last solution premature.

All these questions are too young to be so promptly settled. I believe that I can furnish new data on the Asiatic immigrations to America. The analogies between various Asiatic languages, notably the Malay, and the American languages which I have studied most carefully, lead me to believe in the existence of a primitive and universal language, of which we pick up today only scattered strays. Otherwise, how should one find in India words belonging not only to Malay, but to Latin and to Breton? . . . I earnestly request, therefore, that you do not recoil a priori from the Asiatic hypothesis.

The Salvadorean delegate, Sr. Torrès Caicédo, replied: "In the matter of science, all opinion is admissible, provided it is supported by proof and remains. It seems to me, though, meanwhile, that the great civilizations of Central and South America have a strongly original character, that their languages, their monuments, bear a particular stamp which is neither Scandinavian nor Asiatic, but truly American."

"M. Frédéric de Hellwald, Delegate from Austria, has the floor," announced the chairman. That gentleman arose. First he rendered homage to the zeal and erudition of the Reverend Father Petitot. Then he attacked the notion that the Eskimo could have brought civilization from east Asia to the southern countries of America.

It is not neeessary to precipitate ourselves toward conclusions, but it seems established that the Eskimo and related stocks, whether of Asia or of America, formed a race apart, which one could call a boreal race. Between them and the Indians there does not exist any likeness whatever. They could not have served as intermediaries between the civilized peoples of east Asia and those of America. It is possible that between China and Japan, on the one hand, and Mexico and Peru on the other, there were some direct but accidental communications. Without doubt, a Japanese or Chinese junket could have been driven by storms across the Pacific and cast on the American coast; it has happened more than once in our own times. But civilized man is no wiser than the milieu in which he lives; detached from that milieu, he loses his superiority. What would have happened to some poor fisherfolk or sailors cast on an unknown shore, among barbarian tribes whose language they could not understand? There is not an Asiatic or a European who would have civilized the Indians under these circumstances. Instead, they would have themselves become savages, forgetting their native country and perhaps even their mother tongue, for that is the history of all individuals abandoned or cast on a deserted coast, it is the history of all Robinson Crusoes. Never have these Crusoes served the cause of civilization.

M. Léon de Rosny was again recognized. He bitterly attacked the ideas of the Reverend Father Petitot. Even the official minutes of the Congress referred to it as *une guerre courtoise, mais acharnée.* "All these hypotheses of Asiatic influences on the American civilizations are very piquant," he concluded. "It is the *proof* wherein lies the flaw." Petitot replied heatedly, "I have not come to any final conclusions at all. I do not intend to conclude anything. I ask only that you not judge without having heard."

Here the minutes of the Congress break off discreetly, or the participants lapsed into sullen silence. The next to have the floor was Lucien Adam, who read a lengthy paper reviewing the Fu-Sang theory of an ancient Chinese discovery of America. When he finished, Frédéric de Hellwald rose and observed dryly:

This Fu-Sang legend keeps turning up periodically, as obstinately and as regularly as the Sea Serpent apparition is reported in our journals. Just as no one has ever admitted personally to having studied that animal zoologically, so has no one ever scientifically proved the discovery of America by the Chinese. Dr. Bretschneider several years ago amply refuted this fable, which didn't prevent an English book on it from appearing recently. It is to be feared that the refutation of M. de Rosny and Lucien Adam will not put a stop to the reappearance of the monster. The Congress of Nancy would render a true service to science in declaring that it holds the Fu-Sang theory to be a scientific sea serpent and in forbidding it to infest henceforth the latitudes of Americanism.

7

KON-TIKI
AND THE LINGUISTIC
ACROBATS

THOR HEYERDAHL's vivid adventure narrative, the best seller *Kon-Tiki*, proved that ancient Peruvians could have crossed the Pacific east to west in their prehistoric balsa rafts, a feat once thought to be well nigh impossible. Heyerdahl believes not only that they did this, but that Polynesian population and culture were thus derived from South America, carried about A.D. 500 by the legendary Peruvian culture-hero, the blond god Viracocha and his fellow migrants. Six hundred years later, according to Heyerdahl, "Caucasian-like" but also slightly Mongoloid Kwakiutl Indians from the North American northwest coast invaded Hawaii, merged with the Peruvian migrants, and formed the present Oceanic or Maori-Polynesian race and culture in these islands. He bases this on the resemblance between the pre-Incaic name for Viracocha, said to be "Con-Tici" or "Illa Tici," and the Polynesian god "Tiki"; on what he fancies to be similar art styles in Polynesia and ancient Peru; on early accounts of light-skinned natives on Easter Island, and of fair, bearded culture-heroes in Peru, with fair, bearded, or aquiline-nosed people depicted in South and Central American prehistoric art (whom the Lost Tribes of Israel theorists consider to be Israelites); on the distribution of the sweet potato and the gourd, domesticated on both sides of the Pacific before the European discovery; and on the similarity of art styles between Northwest Coast aboriginal America and Polynesia.

At first glance this is an imposing array of evidence, but it did not dismay American professional anthropologists, who, almost as a body, have constituted for several generations a sort of watchdog committee to guard the unwary public against what the scientists consider hasty theories regarding the origin and prehistoric foreign relationships of the American Indian. With this new threat confronting them, they kept a nervous eye on the list of best-selling books, for every time that a Heyerdahl book made the best ten it meant that new thousands of *Kon-Tiki* and *Aku-Aku* fans were joining the lists of their enemies. If there is anything that an avid adventure-reader hates it is an egghead scholar who primly pours a test tube of cold water on an already brine-soaked blond Viking hero who conquered the roaring Pacific to demonstrate his faith in a dramatic theory, when the spectacled scientists had said it couldn't be done.

Although they should have known better, the anthropologists nevertheless lined up for their turn to attack the Heyerdahl thesis. Perhaps one of the best qualified to do so was the curator of Oceanic ethnology at the Chicago Natural History Museum, Dr. Alexander Spoehr, later director of the famous Bernice P. Bishop Museum in Hawaii, a position his friends sometimes accuse him of accepting to escape the wrath of *Kon-Tiki aficionados* here on the mainland. Dr. Spoehr did not deny that Heyerdahl proved a trip of this kind could be made; he did deny that any migrations of such lasting effect actually took place. The etymology of the Peruvian "Tici" is far from certain, he pointed out, and besides, the occasional chance occurrences of the same word or word element in two unrelated languages is a common phenomenon. Recently I ran across a note of African ethnography that the Akka, a wandering tribe of dwarfs first described by the explorer, Henry Morton Stanley, were called the *Tiki-Tiki* by their neighbors. Are we to infer that they, too, are somehow involved in the Viracocha exodus? As for their skin color, the Polynesians are quite lightly pigmented on body parts not exposed to sunlight and are known to have a Caucasoid-like strain in their racial ancestry. The material cultures of pre-Incaic Peru and of Polynesia were not the same, and what similarities in stonework existed were also found equally strong in Malaysia and Micronesia far to the west. The sweet potato and the gourd do indicate some contact between Old and New Worlds, but this is no evidence for a migration—no more, says Dr. Spoehr, than would lead one to believe that because the "Irish" potato is derived from South America, Irishmen are *ipso facto* migrants from South America also. As for resemblances in art styles between the Pacific islands and South America or the Northwest Coast, "they have never impressed critical students of the area as being alike."

On the contrary, Dr. Spoehr advances an imposing body of adverse evidence: The Polynesian languages belong to the Malayo-Polynesian family stretching across Micronesia and Malaysia to the southeastern Asia island archipelago. The outrigger canoe across this same belt enabled easy migrations from the mainland eastward, and this is confirmed by a series of Oceanic food plants, such as taro, coconut, bananas, and breadfruit, as well as the domesticated pig, linking Polynesia to the Old World rather than the New. And why, asks Dr. Spoehr, if the Polynesians are in large part seafaring Peruvians, are fundamental Peruvian traits like the highly developed textile arts and ceramics not found among them, and if Viracocha and his cohorts were indeed blond or red-headed as claimed, why haven't we found this Caucasoid element in the abundant pre-Inca skeletal remains?

Another distinguished critic of Heyerdahl was Hans Plischke, director of the Institute of Ethnology at the University of Göttingen. Plischke wrote that ever since James Cook's voyages, science has recognized the cultural and ethnic-historical connections of the Polynesians with southeast Asia. Linguistic, physical anthropological, and ethnological as well as historical evidence all support a migration of South Sea islanders eastward from Indonesia into the Pacific; there is a convincing summary, according to Plischke, as early as 1870: George Gerland's *Origin of the Polynesians*. Theories which deny the population movement was from the west rather than from America because of adverse trade winds and currents ignore Malayan seamanship, said Plischke; they knew how to cruise against the wind. According to this author, a native named Tupia, whom Captain Cook took along with him from Tahiti in 1769, could interpret without difficulty not only in New Zealand but also in the Malayan Archipelago, showing an early linguistic relationship when these people were first discovered. Indeed, Plischke added, the word "Tiki" itself is of Malayan origin according to authorities on Indonesian and Marquesan languages.

Dr. Edward Norbeck wrote of Heyerdahl's 821-page book, *American Indians in the Pacific:*

The treatment throughout is opportunistic. Every straw is seized, bent and twisted to suit the author's purposes. Tenuous evidence is pushed beyond reasonable limits; conflicting data are given scant attention or omitted, and the manuscript abounds with incautious statements. The author is both ingenious and ingenuous, and verbal magic is a recurrently used tool. Even the reader who, like this reviewer, is only modestly informed on the areas concerned may find many hundreds of points which he will question or reject.

Probably the only unqualified approval from a professional anthropologist was that of Dr. W. M. Krogman, who, in the *Chicago Sunday Tribune* called it "a learned work, well written, carefully documented and beautifully illustrated. . . . This volume will sail the turbulent seas of scientific evaluation—I

think it will prove seaworthy!" Several anthropological re-
viewers gave Heyerdahl full credit for re-opening and re-
stimulating the problem of trans-Pacific contacts, although they
did not feel that his book actually contributed much toward
its solution. The late Wendell C. Bennett of Yale wrote in the
New York Times that Heyerdahl had introduced a new body
of evidence on Polynesian origins that, because of their quanti-
ty and quality, could not be ignored, but he felt that Heyerdahl
had overstated his case and that the matter was not yet re-
solved, since "there are still serious objections to attributing
total Polynesian origins to the New World." The late Ralph
Linton, also of Yale University, said the time has come to
review the evidence for contact between Oceania and America
during ancient times, but he attacked almost every aspect of
Heyerdahl's method and interpretation.

Heyerdahl, incidentally, was by no means the first to propose
a movement of early culture from Peru to the Eastern Hemisphere. Beginning about the middle of the nineteenth century,
Charles Wolcott Brooks, Japanese consul in San Francisco,
began collecting data on the history of east Asia and possible
communication with the Americas. According to Hubert Howe
Bancroft, who examined Brooks's manuscript, "Origin of the
Japanese Race, and Their Relation to the American Continent,"
the consul recognized striking analogies between the Chinese
and the Peruvians and concluded that the former came originally from Peru. He argued for an east-to-west movement (as
opposed to the opposite direction) on the basis of the difficulty
of bucking the trade winds and currents that pass from Peru
to China; on the other hand, if a large craft were placed before
the wind and set adrift from the Peruvian coast, Brooks said,
there was a strong probability that it would drive straight on
to the southern coast of China.

In 1958, a Mormon named DeVere Baker and three com-
panions drifted sixty-nine days on a raft from California to
Hawaii. Baker failed in his first three tries to break free of
North American coastal currents, but his fourth craft, the

18-by-18-foot nine-ton Lehi IV, equipped with a 20-foot sail, was released off Long Beach, drifted for a time off the Guadalupe Islands, and then caught the trade winds westward. The purpose of the voyage, according to an Associated Press dispatch from Honolulu the day the raft was towed ashore, was to prove "how the world's population migrated and interbred thousands of years ago." According to the newspaper account, more particularly Baker wanted to substantiate *The Book of Mormon*'s account of how the prophet Lehi sailed from the Red Sea to Central America. To do this, Baker is planning, as I write this, to attempt a similar trip by raft from the Persian Gulf eastward to the New World.

Most of the untrained and less inhibited Americanists have dabbled at one time or another, as Thor Heyerdahl did with his Peruvian and Polynesian word lists, in comparative linguistics, blithely unaware of the pitfalls. Augustus Le Plongeon, who spent the last three decades of his colorful life ranting against the leading anthropological authorities in the United States, wrote from tropical Cozumel Island off the coast of Yucatan that the Maya tongue contained words from almost every language, ancient and modern. This was an expectable conclusion for one whose confidence in the historical significance of sound similarities between selected vocabularies was implicit. A Hungarian student of mine once proudly brought me a long list of Finno-Ugrian words that could be very nearly duplicated in modern Yucatec Maya, with identical, closely similar, or at least vaguely comparable meanings. He was convinced of a historical relationship even when, after my own arguments failed, I persuaded him to let me send his paper (he was afraid someone would pirate it) to the best linguistic scholars in the country, all of whom rejected it in short order. Finally I believe I dented his armor by assembling my own list of some fifty near-duplications between *English* and Maya, but if I had shown the two lists to Dr. Le Plongeon he would doubtless have taken both enthusiastically to his bosom.

Here are some of the derivations suggested for the name

Yucatan. The early Spanish historian, Diego Lopez de Cogolludo, wrote that in 1517 the Cordoba expedition, coasting the
peninsula, asked the name of one large town and the natives
answered, "Tectatan," which means "I do not understand."
Receiving this same reply wherever they went, the Spaniards
took it to be the name of the entire country. Yucatan was then
said to be a corruption. John MacKintosh, who in 1836 managed to summarize confidently an orthodox history of the
world, including the story of mankind, in seventeen tiny
printed pages, stated flatly that Shem, the second son of Noah,
had five sons, one of whom, Arphazad, was the father of Salah,
who begat Eber, whose elder son was called Joktan, and that
is whom Jucatan, or Yucatan, is named after. Count Jean
Frederick Waldeck, who began a forty-three-year career as a
Maya archeologist at the age of sixty-six and is said to have
died in Paris as a result of an accident suffered when he turned
his head to look at a pretty girl, first thought that he recognized
in "Yucatan" the name of Yectatan, son of Heberto and father
of Ofir. Somewhat later he discovered that the Reverend Father
Gregorio García, another supporter of the Lost Tribes of Israel
theory, had proposed the same idea in 1607. Whether finding
a prior claim to this hypothesis dampened his own faith in it
we can only guess, but at any rate Waldeck was soon questioning how in the world Tectatan could possibly be confused with
Yucatan, a query that occurs to almost everyone else, too, and
he decided that it was more reasonable to suppose that the
name came instead from the Maya *uyukutan*, "listen to what
they say"—probably in the sense of "Did you ever hear such
crazy talk." In 1905 Rejón García, no relation to Father
Gregorio so far as I know, wrote that Yucatan comes from *y*,
"his," plus *u*, "necklace," *c*, "our" and *atan*, "wife or woman"
—thus the Indians kept demanding of the Spaniards, *Contoon
y u c'atan*, "Sell us necklaces for our wives." How that became
the name of the country is not explained, which seems a weak
link in this chain of already dubious reasoning. Still another
scholar—I have been able to find him referred to only as Sr.

Carillo—thought that the name meant "necklace of the land."

This is a game at which, obviously, any number can play, unhampered by rules for manipulating the words. Take this, from a *Memoire de M. de Paravey sur l'origine japonaise, arabe et basque de la civilisation des peuples du plateau de Bogota*, published in Paris in 1835: The number twenty, says M. de Paravey, is *egueu* in Basque; now *gue* in Muysca, an Indian language of Colombia, means "house," and, the author tells us quite seriously, "without doubt containing twenty persons communally." This identity, he continues, is remarkable, but it is not unique, for "one" in Japanese is *fito*, from which it is easy to derive *fato*, and *fata*, and *bata*, the last of which means "man," with *ata* in Muysca and *bat* in Basque meaning the same thing.

Lucien de Rosny was another word-manipulator of the nineteenth century who presented the following astonishing argument in his *Étude d'Archéologie Américain Comparée*. The word *atl* or *at*, meaning water in Mexican Nahuatl, is also in old Scandinavian; by a transposition of letters, the French have *altérer*, which seems also to be the radical of the Anglo-Saxon *water*, the *w* being no more than a local aspiration. *Atli* was the name of a tenth-century Scandinavian lord. The mountain *Atlas* in Africa, personified in classical mythology as the lord of heaven (*atlao*), also implies the idea of water. Actually the water supports the air, as air supports fire, hence (De Rosny still speaking, I assure you) the physical law of the density of bodies and hence the three myths symbolic of purification. *Atlantic* designates part of the ocean, *Atla* is an ancient Panamanian town at the edge of the Atlantic, and *Utatlan*, a name from the same radical, designates Maya ruins which, M. de Rosny points out triumphantly, are situated between the two oceans! I excavated for Tulane University at Utatlan, in the Guatemala highland at an elevation of about seven thousand feet (a good two or three days' travel by any means except aircraft from either ocean), situated on the top of a steep fortress hill surrounded by almost impassable gorges, with the nearest water several miles away, and a less likely spot to be named after anything having to do with water can scarcely be imagined, unless it was that the Indians were always so thirsty that it was continually on their minds.

Linguistic evidence has been advanced to support just about every theory of American Indian origins, from Egyptian to Carthaginian to Polynesian to Welsh. Thomas Morton in 1637 heard the Indians say, "Pasco-pan," and from this decided that their ancestors were acquainted with the god Pan, thus confirming his belief that they were of Greek and Roman descent. In 1926 Professor Leo Wiener of Harvard published a magnificent volume containing three hundred and twenty-six plates, all but a few of them in color, devoted to the thesis that Maya and Nahuatl languages were derived from the Mandingo of Negro Africa. Some three thousand Maya-Mexican and African words were presented as evidence. In 1883, the Consul General and Chargé d'Affaires of the French Republic to Central America, P. Dabry de Thiersant, in his work, *De l'Origine des Indiens du Nouveau-Monde et de leur Civilisation,* listed sound resemblances between words in Quechua of Peru, Maya of Central America, and Sanskrit. One of the most amusing and devastating attacks on such methods was launched by Edward John Payne in 1899; he produced long lists of striking word similarities between Mexican Nahuatl and Greek, and between Mexican Nahuatl and Latin. "Nothing short of a continuous miracle," said Payne, "could prevent such coincidences." Sixty-three years earlier still, J. MacKintosh, in *The Discovery of America by Christopher Columbus and the Origin of the North America Indian,* sounded the same warning and showed that radical resemblances between Celtic and Algonkin did not mean that the Indians were related to the Irish.

Among all the unrepressed linguistic acrobatics in this general field, I would award first prize to a work published in 1945 at Charlottesville, Virginia: *America: The Background of Columbus,* by Jennings C. Wise. One could choose almost at random from the several hundred pages, but a few examples convey the tone of this astounding book. Wise's usual technique seems to have been to pick one syllable from a word or place name and then to see where else he could find it in an atlas. Thus, he finds it significant that the following places all contain the letters *bra:* "La-bra-dor, the sacred peak of Bra-zo in New Mexico, the Bra-zos in Texas, Bra-za in Argentina next to Bra-zi-la, Bra-za in Austria, and Brahma-poo-t-ra in India." Again, Wise examines the name *America,* and decides that *Amar* is the key to its history: ". . . because the ark of Amaravati was common to the whole earth we find the following place names bearing the Naga-Maya place name America: A-mar-go-za in Na-va-da, 'The Serpent, the Divine, Diva.' Amar-illo in Tejas, 'the Land of Peace' (Texas). Amar-illas in C-u-b-a, 'The Serpent, the Universal Man.' . . . Amar in Syria. S-Amer-ia in Syria. S-amar-kand. S-amar in the Philippines. S-amoa. Amaraka-no-ta-ka in India. . . ." One more example, if you can hold on: "Equally plain is the connection between C-ana-da, 'Christos, Ana, the Divine Ark,' Mont-ana, . . . Gui-a-na, Gui-n-ea. . . . Plainly T-a-na-sa (Tennessee) is the western counterpart of T-a-na-se-rim leading from Burmah to Sin-ga-pore, a relic of the bird's wattle."

Wise further maintained that in A.D. 66, a flotilla of vessels "of unmistakable Graeco-Roman type" appeared in Yucatan. This contact, he notes seriously, explains such Georgia place names as Athens, Rome, Augusta, and Atlanta!

What is it about playing thus with words that is so convincing to the pseudo-scientist and his enthusiastic reading public? No businessman in his right mind would reach a financial decision on the basis of evidence like this; no doctor would dream of diagnosing a case from only one or two chance symptoms; no court in the land will convict a man on circumstantial evidence as meager and as shaky. Yet hundreds of thousands of avid readers of *Kon-Tiki* and *Aku-Aku,* having absorbed several hundred pages of purely adventure narrative, are convinced irrevocably that Thor Heyerdahl and his companions, after their magnificent feats of courage and seamanship, demonstrated beyond all doubt that a Peruvian god named Kon-Tiki was the same as a white chief-god named Tiki mentioned by an old man on an island in the south seas! And this in spite of the fact that Heyerdahl specifically states in an appendix to *Kon-Tiki* that his migration theory "was not necessarily proved" by the successful outcome of his famous voyage.

Why? The average person perhaps unconsciously longs to participate in what he senses must be the intellectual thrill of scientific and scholarly research. And comparative linguistics is a perfectly legitimate, useful approach for him to choose for a study of historical connections. One does not go about it, however, by simply matching words that sound alike. Instead, one analyzes the basic language structure, its fundamental type, the nature of its idioms and its grammar, and the similarity in sound and meaning not only of whole words but also of parts of words, roots, and grammatical forms. A certain number of coincidental sound resemblances must be expected between any two languages, whether they are related or not. Thus, as Dr. Alfred L. Kroeber has pointed out, in the native California language, Yuki, the word *ko* means "go," and *kom* means "come," yet no one has ever suggested that Yuki and English are historically related. Kroeber further reminds us that too close a resemblance between part of the stock of two languages immediately suggests that one borrowed from the other in very recent times, because languages are continually changing, their sounds keep modifying, the word meanings gradually shift, and where historical connection between two tongues is real, "it must be veiled by a certain degree of change or distortion." "Grimm's Law" of changes for Indo-European languages is an example: Latin *p* changes to English *f*, and Latin *d* changes to English *t*. *Ped* becomes *foot*, *pater* becomes *father*; and, further, before one can assume historical connection between two peoples whose languages seem similar, one must also investigate possibilities of various cultural processes like convergence, parallel development, secondary assimilation of form, and many other phenomena that the average person does not have the time or opportunity or inclination to train himself to evaluate by the exacting methods of philological science.

Instead, he seeks his gratification the easy, pleasant way. It is no coincidence that the best-known and most effective advertising phrase for generations has been, "It's easy! It's fun!" We see the same phenomenon in medicine; the tremendous popularity of the medical columnists in newspapers and magazines attests to the public's tremendous yearning to participate in medical knowledge—yet the readers of these articles do not dare risk lives or health on the superficial familiarity with the information they thus absorb. Nor can they risk their own money on a meager knowledge of economics and the market; instead they go to investment consultants, experts who devote their lives to these matters. "A *little* knowledge," almost anyone will tell you, "is a dangerous thing." But not so in a field where there is no obvious risk, where health is not at stake, where money is not put on the line. People do not hesitate to swear allegiance to the Kon-Tiki theory, which is scarcely even discussed in the popular book itself and which, in typical American fashion, they like to see proven by a physical adventure, a competitive sport, the truth of the theory awarded to the winner of a moving struggle of a man against the sea.

—8

THE RIGHTEOUS
AND THE RACISTS

ALONG WITH THE inclination toward linguistic prestidigitation there is also among supporters of the unorthodox theories of American Indian origins a strong concern with theology, which most professional anthropologists consider irrelevant to the subject. Many writers on prehistoric America, however, have somehow or other managed to steer their arguments into religious and theological channels and to use them to support or attack (depending on their particular religious leaning) Roman Catholicism, Judaism, the Church of England, the Church of Jesus Christ of Latter-day Saints, and various Protestant faiths, not to say religion itself. It is rather to be expected that a clergyman of Cotton Mather's time and dedication would find religious meaning here: he wrote in his *Magnalia Christi Americana* (1702) that although we do not know when or how the Indians first became inhabitants of this continent, "yet we may guess that probably the *Devil* decoyed those miserable salvages [*sic*] hither, in hopes that the gospel of the Lord Jesus Christ would never come here to destroy or disturb his absolute empire over them." But among layman an almost universal attributing of religious or supernatural significance to American native prehistory is less expected.

George Jones, Esquire, whose toga-draped bust adorns the frontispiece of his 1843 book describing a Phoenician settling of America, was a devoutly orthodox member of the Church of England, dedicating his work to the Archbishop of Canterbury and waging in it a vigorous war against atheists and any nonbelievers in the Bible, in the prophesies of Isaiah, or in the curse of Noah. The author kept a nervous eye on his Deity at all times, frequently asking forgiveness if he should be in error, and in one passage reminding God that if the author was wrong in his theory, God Himself had put the idea in his head and must therefore make appropriate allowances before judging him too harshly.

Jones alternately scourged the unbelievers and appealed to the strayers. At the end of his book he felt that he had proved his case for a Phoenician origin of American Indian civilizations and somehow or other in doing so he had also routed the forces of evil:

but to the sceptic,—the God-denying atheist, and the labyrinth-lost materialist,—we have . . . encountered them with uncompromising resolution, and upon the Exraic ground of their own selection; and from which they cannot retreat,—they must there remain confounded and defeated; and to the following undebatable, unanswerable conclusion they must be dumb,—or if they speak, be it in humility and repentence: viz.—"those inspired Visions of an unapproached future . . . can be only viewed and received, as the Divine pre-ordinances of ALMIGHTY GOD,—promulgated to a wondering world, from the hallowed lips of His chosen Prophets and Mediators!—Such sacred messengers to Mankind, were Moses, Isaiah, Ezekial, and Daniel;—and the last prophet upon earth,—The Messiah—THE OMNIPOTENT REDEEMER OF THE UNIVERSE!"

Menasseh ben Joseph ben Israel, who wrote in 1650 that the identification of the American aborigines with the Lost Tribes was "the hope of Israel," was chief Rabbi of Amsterdam, and George Jones, who also subscribed to the Lost Tribes theory (to account for the wilder North American tribes), was of the Church of England, yet John D. Baldwin, in his *Ancient America* published in New York in 1872, blamed the whole Israelite hypothesis on the Roman Catholics, calling it "a truly monkish theory" and "a lunatic fancy, possible only to men of a certain class, which in our time does not multiply."

While George Jones and, a few years later, James Kennedy were wielding Indian origin theories to triumph over atheism and antichrists, that cantankerous physician, Augustus Le Plongeon, made his book on this subject a sounding board for one of his many peeves: "It is on this story of the courting of [Maya] Queen Moo by Prince Aac, the murderer of her husband . . . that rests the whole fabric of the Christian religion, which, since its advent in the world, has been the cause of so much bloodshed and so many atrocious crimes." In 1831, a Bible professor, Epaphras Jones, said that his book on the Ten Tribes and the American aborigines was "not made to gratify Man, but to aid the cause of God; therefore, any one is at liberty to approve, or disapprove of the work." This must have put adverse critics at a certain disadvantage.

The preoccupation with religious aspects of what ordinarily appears to be the most secular of subjects is more understandable for the eighteenth and nineteenth centuries, when a group of scientists and public figures, including Voltaire and Louis Agassiz, had rejected the single-origin theory of man and thereby pitted science and reason against church doctrine, than in our century, but there still seems to be a fairly strong religious motivation in many of these studies today, even outside the Church of Jesus Christ of Latter-day Saints, whose *Articles of Faith for the Book of Mormon* officially embrace the American Israelites into Mormon doctrine. For example, James Churchward, the widely read exponent of the Lost Continent of Mu, closes the 1931 edition of his book with these lines: "The elements having released the soul from its bondages, the soul— being governed by the same Divine Law as the elements—must also return whence it came. Coming from 'The Great Source' the glorious triumphant end of man's soul must be—*its return to God.*"

Just what possible relevance this statement has to the book that precedes it is not at all clear to many readers, but there it is, as if its author simply felt compelled to say something theological. In some cases the authors themselves seem puzzled by their apparent religious motivations, and try halfheartedly to justify them. For example, Jennings C. Wise, who wrote *America: The Background of Columbus* in 1945, seemed suddenly to realize that his religious aims needed explanation: "In seeking to bring the fundamentals of Christianity into complete accord with modern scientific findings, the object of the author, however, was not one of a partisan religious nature. His motive was to make the bitter experiences of vanished races yield for the guidance of the thoughtful, lessons of value not to be found in the current type of so-called 'legitimate history.' "

Writings on these matters by members of the Ancient Mystical Order Rosae Crucis (known as the AMORC), the Rosicrucian Fellowship—apparently a quite distinct if not a rival organization—the Theosophical Society, and the Lemurian Fellowship are all heavily tinged with religious implications. The Rosicrucian Order is non-sectarian, but it is devoted to spritual as well as natural laws and its purpose is to "enable all to live in harmony with the creative, constructive Cosmic forces for the attainment of health, happiness, and peace." Max Heindel, who seems to have been the spiritual leader of the Rosicrucian Fellowship—its headquarters are in Oceanside, California, whereas the AMORC headquarters are in San Jose—calls the Rosicrucian cosmo-conception "Mystic Christianity," and although he departs extensively from orthodox Christian theology in his interpretations of Theosophist and related doctrines, he constantly returns to the Bible, to the lordship of Jehovah, and the mission of Jesus. The Theosophical Society lists among its objects the study of ancient and modern religions, and in its writings one finds frequent references to the One Universal Deity, the unknown and invisible

Lotus panel animated by human figures, from sculptured chamber wall of the Great Ballcourt at Chichen Itza, Yucatan. The same motif was used in Hindu-Buddhist art. *After A. P. Maudslay.*

(Courtesy Oxford University Press)

Personages holding lotus scepters or staffs and seated in almost identical positions, one leg tucked under, the other hanging over side of throne.

Left: Khasarpana, India. *After B. Bhattacharyya, illustrated by G. F. Ekholm.*

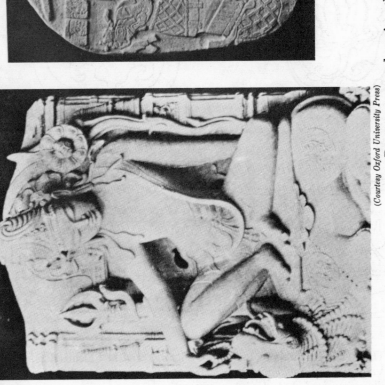

(Courtesy Oxford University Press)

Personages seated on tiger throne.

Left: Stone sculpture, Mahoba, India. *After B. Bhattacharyya, illustrated by G. F. Ekholm.*

Right: Sculptured slab, Palace House E, Palenque, Mexico. *After A. P. Maudslay.*

The water lily motif in India (*left column*) and at Chichen Itza, Yucatan (*right column*). *After R. Heine-Geldern and G. F. Ekholm, illustrated by J. Imbelloni.*

ALL, the inner God, and similar sacred titles, although by and
large they seem much more oriented toward Hindu beliefs and
practices than toward Christian or Judaic.

Racist and nationalist issues, too, have somehow crept into
this topic. We recognize variations on old familiar themes. Dr.
H. W. Magoun, in his introduction to a lengthy linguistic treatise by T. S. Denisen, the amateur philologist, decided that the
Old World emigrants who first reached the Americas in prehistoric times were probably Aryans. "They could hardly have
been anything else. They were white and they were warriors
and they sailed the sea with confidence. They were, therefore,
masterful men. They were in search of new and better homes,
and when they found what satisfied them, they remained there.
Now, these are all Aryan traits, and they have been through
the ages. The Semites migrate also: but it is usually the result
of compulsion. . . . Some necessity that compels obedience
drives them forth. . . ." Epaphras Jones, a Bible professor,
wrote in 1831 that anyone "conversant with the European
Jews and the Aborigines of America . . . will perceive a great
likeness in color, features, hair, aptness to cunning, dispositions for roving, &c."

First prize for modern racism in this particular field must go
to Lewis Spence, well-known champion of the Lost Atlantis
theory, who declared in 1924 that the first Atlanteans to bring
civilization to Europe were Cro-Magnon; then:

If a patriotic Scotsman may be pardoned the boast, I may say that
I devoutly believe that Scotland's admitted superiority in the mental and spiritual spheres springs almost entirely from the prepon-
derant degree of Cro-Magnon blood which certainly runs in the
veins of her people, whose height and cranial capacity, as well as
other physical signs, show them to be mostly of Cro-Magnon race.
England, too, undoubtedly draws much of her sanity, her physical
prowess and marked superiority in the things of the mind from
the same source, and if much of her blood be Iberian, is not that too
Atlantean, and has that admixture not pre-eminently endowed her
with the greatest poets who ever touched the harp? To an admixture of Cro-Magnon and Iberian blood we owe the genius of

Shakespeare and Burns, Massinger and Ben Jonson. Milton, Scott, and, to come to our own times, Mr. H. G. Wells and Mr. Galsworthy are almost purely Cro-Magnon—indeed our literary types strongly resemble the carefully designed bust of a Cro-Magnon man executed under scientific supervision by a distinguished Belgian sculptor.

Thor Heyerdahl's book supporting his Kon-Tiki hypothesis, *American Indians in the Pacific*, attacks the idea that migrations of peoples from Asia and Indonesia passed through Melanesia or Micronesia to Hawaii and the islands of Polynesia. He accounts for Negroid traits among Polynesians as carried by Melanesian slaves or laborers brought there by predominantly Caucasoid Polynesians who came from Peru and the American Northwest Coast, areas which Heyerdahl decided on after searching the Americas for "intelligent" and Caucasoid peoples. Among the Kwakiutl of the Northwest Coast he found Polynesian-like and Caucasoid traits, including "mental traits." Dr. Edward Norbeck, the anthropologist, commented in his review of the book for a professional journal, "It will be difficult for many persons to avoid reading racism from this work."

The Lost Tribes of Israel theory of the peopling of America has also provided a sounding board for racist, nationalistic, and anti-Semitic voices. Gregorio García, in the latter part of the sixteenth century, devoted the greater part of his *Origen de los Indios* to a defense of this theory, in the course of which, according to Bancroft, he pointed out that the Indians were cowards like the Jews; that the Indians, like the Jews, did not readily receive the Christian faith and were therefore persecuted and were rapidly approaching extermination; that the Jews were ungrateful for the many blessings God bestowed on them, just as the American Indians did not appreciate Spanish kindness; that the Jews and Indians were notoriously uncharitable to poor and sick, both were naturally given to idolatry; both were liars, despicable, incorrigible, and vicious; both were "fit only for the lowest kind of labor, the Jews preferring the flesh-pots of Egypt and a life of bondage to heavenly manna and the promised land, while the Indians chose a life of freedom and a diet of roots and herbs rather than what the Spaniards offered them." One would think that at least this last remark would have given even Father Gregorio pause for thought, but obviously it did not.

Many members of the Church of Jesus Christ of Latter-day Saints also have strong racist attitudes toward all dark-skinned peoples, as I found to my astonishment when I left the Deep South one summer to teach at the University of Utah, which is non-sectarian and has about half-gentile and half-Mormon student body. The prejudice stems from *The Book of Mormon*, which declares that when Lehi's sons, Laman and Lemuel, rebelled, God cursed them and their American Indian (Lamanite) descendants with a dark skin. Several students in my Utah classes maintained stoutly that Negroes have thicker skulls than whites, and that therefore they have inferior brains; correlating thick skulls with dark skin, they decided that Indians, too, were handicapped in mentality. This does not mean that the Mormons have abused either Indians or Negroes—quite the contrary. As the non-Mormon Thomas F. O'Dea shows in his most sympathetic book, *The Mormons*, the church from the first conceived as part of its task the reconversion of the Indians that they might once again become a "white and delightsome people," and he says that a generally favorable attitude toward the Indian has marked the Mormon outlook ever since, an attitude that on several occasions has aroused suspicion and hostility among their white gentile neighbors.

Strong racist opinions appear also in Max Heindel's *The Rosicrucian Cosmo-Conception* (1929), where he derives Negroes "and the savage races with curly hair" from the Lost Continent of Lemuria (Mu), occupied during an earlier, more primitive stage of human development, and Jews from a later epoch on Atlantis, when human beings were "governed more by . . . Cunning than by Reason." According to Heindel, the Jews lost out because they intermarried with other Atlantean races, "thus bringing inferior blood into their descendants" and consequently they could not make the racial transition from Cunning to Reason. "In them the race-feeling is so strong that they distinguish only two classes of people: Jews and Gentiles. They despise the other nations and are in turn despised by them for their cunning, selfishness and avarice. It is not denied that they give to charity, but it is principally if not exclusively, among their own people and rarely internationally. . . . The rejection of Christ by the Jews was the supreme proof of their thralldom to Race." There is a good deal more of this sort of talk which Heindel thinks "the Western peoples" should heed, "that they may be taught a lesson by the awful example of the Jewish Race as recorded in the Old Testament." It is the Aryan races, of course, in whom Heindel believes Reason is being evolved to perfection.

If anyone is startled by this reasoning, he will get an even greater jolt when he delves further into mystic reconstructions of human evolution and race history. They differ in details among the various orders, but all follow the same general outline and point of view, and one can obtain a sort of average from Mme Blavatsky's *The Secret Doctrine*, A. P. Sinnett's *Esoteric Buddhism*, Claude Falls Wright's *Modern Theosophy*, and Max Heindel's *The Rosicrucian Cosmo-Conception*. During four main periods "the life-wave" has moved from one chain of worlds and one globe to another—the Saturn Period, the Sun Period, the Moon Period, and the present or Earth Period. The Moon, now a cold and dead "planet," is doomed for long ages to be ever pursuing the Earth. "Constantly *vamperized* by her child, she revenges herself on it by soaking it through and through with the nefarious, invisible and poisoned influence which emanates from the occult side of her nature. . . . And like all ghouls or vampires, the moon is the friend of the sorcerers and the foe of the unwary." Human evolution actually began in the fiery material of the Sun that later formed the Earth. The mystics believe that somehow "man himself built his first mineral body, assisted by the Lords of Form." The Earth has passed through, first, a series of "revolutions" which recapitulated the Saturn-Earth-Moon sequence, followed by a series of epochs, the third of which was the Lemurian, the fourth the Atlantean, and the fifth the present or Aryan Epoch. In the Lemurian Epoch, Man was helped "to take the first tottering steps of Evolution," as the Rosicrucian, Max Heindel, expressed it, by beings much further advanced than man along the path of evolution; they came from Venus and Mercury "on the errand of love to guide our humanity."

The mystics recognize sixteen "root-races." The first of these, including the Negroes, became the "Seed" for the seven Atlantean races in the succeeding epoch, but the Lemurians— or, as occultists prefer to say, the *forms* inhabited by the Lemurians—degenerated into the savages and anthropoids of the present day. The fourth root-race was of Atlantis, which rose where the Atlantic Ocean now is, after volcanic cataclysms destroyed the Lemurian continent. The Toltecs were the third Atlantean sub-race, and this aspect of mystic theory brings it for the first time in direct identification with an American Indian tribe, for the Toltecs were a prehistoric ethnic group of Mexico, their capital at Tula in what is now Hidalgo. According to Heindel, the Toltecs developed their memory far beyond its present powers, calling on it for experience when they had to make some decision. The Semites were the fifth of the seven Atlantean sub-races, but they lost out because of their avarice, though they were ancestors of the Aryans of the present (in occultist thought, the fifth) epoch.

In mystic theory, two more races will evolve, one of them Slavs, including the Russian people, from whom will descend the last of the Aryan Epoch's seven races. From the people of the United States will develop the last of all the races in this evolution, and they will hold sway in the beginning of the Sixth Epoch. After that there will be nothing "that can properly be called a Race." It is small wonder that the mystics view the present world developments with a certain degree of equanimity, not to say smug satisfaction. Since mystic beliefs are allegedly derived largely from the Himalayas, India, and Tibet, one wonders why more of the peoples of this region of the world do not throw in their lot more decidedly with the United States as opposed to Russia. It is not stated in the *Rosicrucian Cosmo-Conception* whether the Asiatic occultists share these beliefs in the future with their American colleagues.

What, indeed, is the connection between religion, racism, nationalism, and the origin of the American Indian? Any one of the writers referred to here would doubtless aver that his information simply led him to these matters and that in all honesty he could not ignore the results. But looking at these writers as a group, we have noted that for some of them American Indian prehistory favors one church, for others some other faith, and for still others a completely different set of religious or theological or racial or nationalistic beliefs. The only thing really that they have in common is an inordinate interest in religion, race, or national patriotism.

In recent years religious scholars have begun to state their religious or theological beliefs as hypotheses, then to limit themselves to empirical methods of testing them. Some Mormons, particularly, are submitting their religious beliefs about the American Indian past to the test of archeology, and as long as they stay within the rules of science, at least some gentile anthropologists have shown themselves willing and eager to co-operate. Physical anthropologists and psychologists, too, have demonstrated continuing interest in testing theories about race—but through empirical methods, not by quoting holy books.

——9

THE MYSTICS:
CONCLUSION

*When a man's knowledge is not in order, the more
of it he has the greater will be his confusion.*
—HERBERT SPENCER

MARTIN GARDNER, in his excellent book on
Fads & Fallacies in the Name of Science, found that the crank
pseudo-scientists described in his first chapter hold certain
traits in common. First, the crank works in almost total isolation from his fellows, and second, he has a tendency toward
paranoia likely to be exhibited in five ways: he considers himself a genius; he regards his colleagues as ignorant blockheads;
he believes himself unjustly persecuted and discriminated
against; he chooses the greatest scientists and the best-estab-
lished theories to attack; and he writes in a complex jargon.
Most advocates of what the professional anthropologists consider "the wild theories" of American Indian origins qualify
as pseudo-scientists in all these criteria and share some other
characteristics as well. Orthodox anthropologists complain that
these people make no effort to organize their thoughts or their
data in an orderly fashion—with the possible exception of

Lewis Spence and Ignatius Donnelly—that one thing leads to another indefinitely, that they seek no goals other than religious ones and are therefore not interested in proofs, consequently not in empirical methods.

The historian, Hubert Howe Bancroft, for example, wrote of the Abbé Brasseur de Bourbourg, whom he greatly admired in spite of the Abbé's turning from a lifetime of scholarship to an old age of irresponsible speculations about Atlantis and Mexican Indian mysticism:

It is not my intention to enter the mazes of Brasseur's argument here; once in that labyrinth there would be small hope of escape. His *Quatre Lettres* are a chaotic jumble of facts and wild speculation that would appall the most enthusiastic antiquarian; the materials are arranged with not the slightest regard for order; the reader is continually harassed by long rambling digressions—literary no-thoroughfares as it were, into which he is beguiled in the hope of coming out somewhere, only to find himself more hopelessly lost than ever; for mythological evidence, the pantheons of Phoenicia, Egypt, Hindustan, Greece, and Rome are probed to their most obscure depths. . . .

Within two days after one of the Tulane University archeological expeditions to Yucatan was announced we received from Boston a three-page, single-spaced typewritten letter, no paragraph of which made any sense relative to any other, or for that matter within itself, yet like doubletalk it almost did if you read it fast enough. It reminded me unpleasantly of a long evening a University of Georgia colleague and I spent, over twenty years ago, listening to a mystic's earnest and unbroken comments on several hundred lantern slides of symbols from ancient inscriptions; when he finished we realized that it had all led up to absolutely nothing. Here, verbatim, are three of our Boston correspondent's twenty-eight paragraphs:

In the overall problem; so thoroughly obscured by the destruction of records et al by Spanish faction; there is a small amount of material which even Spinden would not (or could not get it published) which bears on the overall problem.

Hence the deterioration to 'Human Sacrifice' in Mexico; after the Anselm 'Dogma' & Thomas Aquinas Dogma got publicised after 1000 A.D. The 'Donus Scotus' faction opposed that notion 'On this side' of the pond; but had less use for 'Greed of Spain' after 1492; hence the famous feat of John Decosa Guidio de Nina of Columbus; and the 'Piri Reis' affair; which in turn (after his pal in The Porte passed on; he showed up in Flanders as the Sailor of Sir Thomas More: cited in A Short History of England:—by Greene; indexed under Sir Thomas More. The natural following down through Tom Paine is obvious; and the reaction to 'Age of reason' is well known.

As a matter of simple fact: a bale of Prime Mink skins from Northern Canada was worth more in 'Harems' (Courts of England a la Louis VIXth etc etc) that its equivalent weight in Gold; which as a family legend sure amuses us even in 1957. Which angle no HONEST historian ever would print in explaining the Gold of NO value (it was NOT legal merchandize in Maya-Aztec-Inca areas) but the sequel in Ben Johnson's 'The Alchemist' london England 1610 (I have the 1880 era reprint) is THE proof.

Although this gibberish is clearly beyond the lunatic fringe, it illustrates very well certain characteristics of the mystics who delve in American Indian lore. It is couched in what its author considers scientific or, more probably, historical jargon; it speaks knowingly of other persons' inept misconceptions; it hints darkly that certain leading scholars are suppressing information; although completely disorganized it nevertheless reflects a certain amount of serious reading on the part of the writer; so far as I can tell it says absolutely nothing.

Even Thor Heyerdahl, whose bestselling *Kon-Tiki* and *Aku-Aku* earned him a well-deserved reputation as a master of adventure narrative, when he attempted to explain his theories in a separate scholarly book, *American Indians in the Pacific*, used 763 pages of text to present a fairly simple hypothesis and a not overwhelming amount of evidence in its behalf. His reviewer in *American Antiquity*, Dr. Edward Norbeck, complained: ". . . it may be said that this work is poorly organized and extremely repetitious. One gets the impression that a mass of notes or the rough draft of a manuscript somehow or another got published."

It does not help matters with professionals, who are prone to write in what often seems an unnecessarily drab style, that their less inhibited rivals embellish undocumented historical reconstructions in the headiest prose. Phoenician sailors landing in prehistoric America according to the George Jones version "arrived in joyous gladness" and

". . . still the star-tracery on the azure wall of the external Dome, and their Apollo daily sinking on his Western couch, and with his last glance, beckoning them as it were, still to follow on his path,— this knowledge and their Religious adoration, directed them in safety to that Virgin land where the glorious Sun from Creation's dawn, had never beamed upon a human foot-print, until their own had kissed the untouched Floridian Shore! There Flora and her attendant Nymphs in all their peerless beauty, and Nature's own attire, were grouped on every hill; from their coloured lips smiling Welcome breathed forth her ceaseless incense from every mound and valley, which waft on Zephyr's wings enrapt with health and gladness the approaching Sons and Daughters of a distant Sea, whose wild songs of praise to gorgeous Apollo were borne by their Orient and faithful envoy to the wave-clad Shore. . . .

Ten years after George composed these rapturous lines, his Phoenician theory was taken up by Pablo Felix de Cabrera of Guatemala, who subscribed to a tall tale about an unlikely world voyager named Votan, said to have been descended from Hercules, a traveler of no mean proportions himself. When Don Pablo decided that Votan was assassinated by his brother Typhon, he raged:

Impious and inhuman Typhon, may thy memory be accursed with interminable hatred, for daring to stain thy murderous hands with the blood of thy brother and thy king, thus leaving to posterity the execrable example, of a twofold crime so horrible: thy ambition caused a polished people to tear asunder the most sacred bonds, to precipitate themselves into the greatest atrocities, to tarnish the glory of their ancestors, and to disgrace their nation!

For James Churchward, the hummingbirds on the Lost Continent of Mu darted "hither and thither from flower to flower" and "feathered songsters in bush and tree vied with each other in their sweet lays," and for almost all chroniclers of Atlantis or Mu the bowels of earth rumbled and roared as subterranean fires blasted asunder the entire continent and the sea pounded in to still an ancient civilization forever, or words to that effect. It seems well nigh impossible to resist this way of writing about Atlantis. Even Captain Gilbert Rude, in a 1940 U.S. Naval Institute article otherwise devoted to such prosaic matters as echo soundings, taut-wire methods, box lines, and incline angles, could shift gears rapidly into the Lost Continent idiom:

The once thriving Atlantean seaports are now cities of silence, their builders forgotten. Where throbbed the pulse of a mighty civilization, the denizens of the deep now lazily swim. Palaces, once the scene of youth and laughter, are but hollow tombs; temples no longer resound to priestly words of wisdom. The magnificence and wealth that was Atlantis perished in a single night in the final great catastrophe. The island continent was rocked by earthquakes, volcanoes belched destruction, and seismic sea waves lent their pounding might. The land slowly settled beneath the seething waters to become the continent of mystery.

To historians and social scientists, who try to eliminate from their writing what they call "value judgments," this lush phraseology is repugnant and suspect. As for the serious occult writers, who leave the light and fancy styles to their disciples, their idiom is so specialized that even when the modern professional anthropologist makes a conscientious effort to read and digest what they have to say he frequently gives up and admits defeat. Readers of the *Rosicrucian Digest* and the *Theosophical Quarterly* do not seem to experience this difficulty. The articles in these journals cover a wide range of styles and complexity, but the most simply worded do not hesitate to quote the great mystic masters—like H. Spencer Lewis or Mme H. P. Blavatsky (known to the initiated as

H.P.B.)—writing at their highest esoteric pitch. Here is an H.P.B. excerpt from the *Quarterly:*

Parabrahman, the One Reality, the Absolute, is the field of Absolute Consciousness, i.e., that Essence which is out of all relation to conditioned existence, and of which conscious existence is a conditioned symbol. But once that we pass in thought from this (to us) Absolute Negation, duality supervenes in the contrast of Spirit (or Consciousness) and Matter, Subject and Object. Spirit (or Consciousness) and Matter are, however, to be regarded, not as independent realities, but as the two symbols or aspects of the Absolute, Parabrahman, which constitute the basis of conditioned Being whether subjective or objective. The Manifested Universe, therefore, is pervaded by duality, which is, as it were, the very essence of its *Ex*-istence as Manifestation. But just as the opposite poles of Subject and Object, Spirit and Matter, are but aspects of the One Unity in which they are synthesized, so, in the Manifested Universe, there is "that" which links Spirit to Matter, Subject to Object. This something, at present unknown to Western speculation is called by Occultists, Fohat. It is the "bridge" by which the Ideas existing in the Divine Thought are impressed on Cosmic Substance as the Laws of Nature . . . the dynamic energy of Cosmic Ideation.

The Theosophist Atlantis champion, Eugen Georg, concludes thus *The Adventure of Mankind,* a 1931 book devoted in large part to considering Atlantean America:

The Way is at an end.

The cosmic age is ended. The eternal rhythm has passed into equilibrium: the omnipotent Demiurge made relative-absolute, transitory-timeless, imperfect-perfect. The longing for equilibrium is fulfilled. The static has replaced the dynamic. The realm of peace and rest has now returned. The world consciousness has submerged in the holy night of Brahma.

Such is the essence of the great mystery!

Such is the meaning of the equilibrium!

This is the sentence from the magic entropy:

THE EVOLUTION OF THE WORLD STRIVES FOR A MAXIMUM OF LOVE!

THE END

Volume XII of the Rosicrucian Library is introduced by the Rosicrucian Press in these words:

Beneath the rolling, restless seas lie the mysteries of forgotten civilizations. Swept by the tides, half buried in the sands, worn away by terrific pressure are the remnants of a culture little known to our age of today. Where the mighty Pacific now rolls in a majestic sweep of thousands of miles, there was once a vast continent. This land was known as Lemuria, and its people as Lemurians. . . . If you are a lover of mystery, of the unknown, the weird—read this book—remember, however, this book is *not fiction*, but based on facts, the result of extensive research.

Mme Blavatsky, the late spiritual leader of the Theosophists, maintained stoutly that the "Secret Doctrine teaches history— which, although esoteric and traditional, is none the less, more reliable than profane history. . . ."

Lewis Spence wrote on the first page of *The Problem of Atlantis:* "A hypothesis must, in any case, stand or fall by the nature of the proof brought to its support, and this I have sought to make of a character as unimpeachable as the very difficult circumstances admit of." On the last page of the same book, though, he wrote:

But however poor my testimony, the intuition which inspired it remains powerful and irrefragable, indestructible, indeed, as the world-memory of that ancient and original culture I have attempted to unveil. Yes, there is more, much more, than mere material proof to be considered in relation to such questions as that which we have been discussing. Atlantis sleeps beneath the seas. But not reason alone, nor the apparatus of scholarship, will, in the end, serve to probe her ancient mysteries. Men of insight have written of strange visions, and of stranger supernatural communication they have been vouchsafed regarding her pristine life.

What kind of science fiction is this? ask the exasperated professionals. How can you profess the scientific method in one breath, but assign ultimate authority to world memory and supernatural communication in another? They cannot understand why the Mormon, Lewis Edward Hills, writing on American archeology in 1924, would devote so much effort to "scientific" location of Nephite place names in Mexico when he eventually heeded a supernatural voice that spoke to him and told him where to look on his Rand McNally map. They are helpless before the Bible professor Epaphras Jones's simple way out of the difficulty of getting the Israelites to the New World: "The Ten Tribes were to be scattered all over the world. God could accomplish this in his own way—Isaiah 11th." They cannot fathom what prompted Robert B. Stacy-Judd to attach supernatural significance to the simple occurrence which he described in his book on *The Ancient Mayas*. Visiting an archeological camp at Uxmal, after a gay party at which considerable quantities of rum were consumed by all present, Stacy-Judd and the archeologist-in-charge passed most of the night talking "as only two men do in silent places." Later, in the brilliance of the silvery moonlight, "spontaneously without premeditation, each turned on the instant and faced the other. Then each, with right hand on the left shoulder, bowed to the other, bending forward from the hips." This, Stacy-Judd explained breathlessly, was an ancient Mayan salutation, a custom thousands of years old, recorded in Mayan works of the southern area, but not yet discovered where they were in northern Yucatan. To his archeologist host the custom was known, but Stacy-Judd had been ignorant of it. "What motivated the simple gesture? Were the inspired souls of that vanished race present, and in sympathy with our quest? Realizing the charmed life I bore in the face of the many adventures and experiences which befell me, especially after I left Uxmal, I cannot help but feel their protective influence was ever at my side."

Thor Heyerdahl's *Aku-Aku* always manages to give the impression that some strange and secret forces lurk about Easter Island, its natives, and the scientists studying there. *Time* magazine said that the book "has travelogue overtones of mystery and menace that seldom seem justified by the events described." Nigel Nicolson wrote in the *New Statesman:* "What is disconcerting about his method is his habit of accepting the romantic explanation of still puzzling facts."

The late supreme executive and Imperator of the Rosicrucian Order, H. Spencer Lewis, announced to the reader what he should expect in one of his books: "Rosicrucians . . . do not depend upon the rules of science for the discovery and test of natural laws and principles. They have their own way by which they may prove the truth or worthiness of a principle, and this method permits them to quickly come to the proper conclusion and with less likelihood of misjudgment than by the scientific method."

Professional anthropologists admit a certain amount of envy for a research method that permits theory to fit hypothesis so conveniently. Stacy-Judd, when he needed to account for five different populations in Eurasia and the Americas, did so simply by stating that Atlantis underwent five different subsidences and upheavals before it finally disappeared. Still, although bewildered by what seems to them to be an inability to distinguish between empiricism and intuition, offended by the lush idiom, provoked by the often bitter charges leveled at them in print by the amateurs, and repelled by the nationalistic, racist, and religious motives so often apparent in these writings, anthropologists today do not believe that the "wild theorists" are all deliberately dishonest—only those few who claim actually to have discovered ancient tablets or to have seen lost cities which disappeared again before the public could examine them. They look on the mystics rather as addicts to the sign, the picture, the form, and the word, and to the intoxicating subject matter of ruined cities, lost tribes, and drowned continents.

Mme Alice Le Plongeon's intimate friend, to whom she intrusted her secret archeological notes as she was dying, interrupts voluminous letters telling what she knew of these records with these almost wholly irrelevant words: "Are you interested in symbols? Or in the tales of the Lost Atlantis? I believe firmly that the Mayas originally came from the Island of

Atlantis, the Azore Islands being the peaks of the mountain range now submerged." Jennings C. Wise believes that even the shape of continents may be somehow symbolic. In 1945 he wrote: "Today we note that a glaciation occurred in the Secondary when the old bird-shaped continent assumed the Jurassic form. Knowing the implication of the Phoenix and the egg shown in the mouth of the Graeco-Egyptian *Cenubis*, we cannot fail to note the symbolic form of the bird-shaped continent of the Primary."

Professionals consider these people dangerous only to the extent that their extremely popular writings persuade so many intellectually unwary people that research is simply a process of manipulating facts, intuition, and imagination in approximately equal parts. It disturbs them to realize that, as Lewis Spence himself declared, no amount of scientific protestation seems capable of shaking the world-wide conviction of the former existence of Atlantis. No one, said a critical editor of the *Dialogues*, knew better than Plato how to invent "a noble lie." Yet the world, "like a child, has readily, and for the most part unhesitatingly accepted the tale of the Island of Atlantis." A further facet of this entire situation that the professional anthropologists deplore is the tendency for men who seem otherwise quite sound and respected in some other profession to go overboard on the "wild" theories of American Indian beginnings. Neuman, McCulloh, Le Plongeon, and Elliot Smith were doctors of medicine, James Kennedy was a lawyer, Harold S. Gladwin a businessman, Thor Heyerdahl an amateur zoologist, Brasseur de Bourbourg a priest, T. S. Denisen a printer, Thomas A. Willard a battery manufacturer, Rufus Dawes a politician.

W. H. Dall wrote in 1885:

Volumes have been filled with the most enthusiastic rubbish by men on whose ability and sanity in other matters, nothing has ever thrown a doubt. Fortunately the era of such speculations is passing away. . . . The "ten lost tribes" still linger with us, and doubtless will continue to do so for some time, probably becoming in their turn the subject of investigation by psychologists interested in aberrant mental phenomena . . . [but] the day is not far distant when men possessed by absurd anthropological hobbies will not longer be patiently permitted to ventilate them before scientific bodies, but will be placed on the same list with the squarers of circles and the discoverers of perpetual motion.

Moreover, the professional scientist winces because he realizes that the public will pour financial support into the most fantastic schemes when these are presented in the richly exciting idiom of Lost Continents and Lost Tribes, and dignified by pseudo-scientific expositions of symbolism and mysticism that are so much more palatable than the bland fare he usually offers. E. D. Merrill wrote in the *American Scholar* in 1936:

The subject affords a permanent source of copy for popular writers, who consistently overstress the similarities and assumed similarities between early civilizations of the two hemispheres. "Aztec Link to Chinese Seen," "Peruvian Mummies Point to Lost Continent," and similar headlines too often betray the fact that some enterprising explorer of Mexico, Yucatan, Central America, Bolivia, or Peru, or his press agent, is preparing to lure the public into providing further funds for the support of future raids into the wilds of nature and fiction.

It chagrins the professional scholar, whose books are usually subsidized because they find no popular market, that small fortunes are made by the publishers and authors of mystical nonsense. The latest postcard announcing one of these has just reached me:

THE MISSING LINKS OF HISTORY
2nd Enlarged Book
By B. J. Harrington

Bringing History, Science and Religion into
Closer Alignment

Spanning the Creator God Period 200,000 B.C.—shedding considerable light on a previous civilization rivaling our own.
Explaining Many Mysteries.
Masonic History from First Advent of Man to Present Day.

First American Indian Colony 148,000 B.C.
Akkadian Empire Known to Have Existed in 114,000 B.C.
Phoenicians Traded with Mayans 3104 B.C.
America Thousands of Years Older than Egypt.
Egyptian Burials in Mexico.

300 Pages   65 Illustrations

$3.50 Post Paid
Your Book Store or
RAINBOW PUBLISHING CO.
3819 Walnut Street
Kansas City 11, Mo.

Those who have read numbers of these fast-selling books
attest that they lack literary merit and in many cases even the
lurid subject matter is presented in a drab fashion. It must be,
then, the subject matter itself that draws the mystics in rav-
enous thousands: the words History, Science, and Religion,
Mysteries, Masonic, Akkadian Empire, Phoenicians and Maya,
Egypt, and 200,000 B.C. Yet to the anthropologist, the Bering
Strait hypothesis and its implications embrace one of the greatest sagas of all human history. He points out that Man was an
essentially tropical animal and had to free himself from his
southern habitat and economy; through perseverance, invention, and courage he adapted himself to the forbiddingly different Inner Asiatic and north Siberian plains, steppes, and
tundras, becoming a grasslands big-game hunter with his stone-
tipped spears and throwing sticks.

This revolution was one of the most dramatic developments
in the history of mankind, say the scientists, and the job of
seeking the powerful motives that impelled Man, an essentially
conservative creature, to move, a few miles here, a few more
there, a generation here, a century there, until he found and
populated an entire new pair of continents not discovered again
for thousands of years, and built there some of the world's
greatest ancient civilizations, should be to professional and
amateur alike a thrilling detective story based on an imaginative plot, with dramatic as well as convincing actors. However,

the scientist has not competed seriously for the reading public; the average professional anthropologist cannot or will not write the kind of book that people in any great numbers will want to read. For the most part he has surrendered this function, usually somewhat condescendingly, to the journalist, the travel-book writer, the sensationalist, and the devoted mystic, all of whom will prefer, any day, a lost continent, a lost tribe, or a lost city, to Lo the Poor Indian plodding through the snow and the centuries to his cultural destiny.

REFERENCES

GENERAL

BALDWIN, JOHN D. *Ancient America*. New York: Harper & Brothers, 1872.

BANCROFT, HUBERT HOWE. *The Native Races*, Vol. V: *Primitive History*. San Francisco: The History Co., 1886.

BRADFORD, ALEXANDER W. *American Antiquities and Researches into the Origin and History of the Red Race*. New York: Dayton & Saxton, 1841.

BRAUNSCHWEIG, JOHANN DAN. VON. *Ueber die Alt-Amerikanischen Denkmäler*. Berlin: G. Reimer, 1840.

BRINE, LINDESAY. *Travels amongst American Indians: Their Ancient Earthworks and Temples*. London: Sampson Low, Marston & Co., 1894.

BRINTON, DANIEL G. *American Hero-Myths*. Philadelphia: H. C. Watts & Co., 1882.

DIXON, ROLAND B. *The Building of Cultures*. New York: Charles Scribner's Sons, 1928.

DRAKE, SAMUEL G. *The Book of the Indians; or, Biography and History of the Indians of North America, from its First Discovery to the Year 1841*. 9th ed. Boston: Benjamin B. Mussey, 1845.

GARDNER, MARTIN. *Fads & Fallacies in the Name of Science.* New York: Dover Publications, Inc., 1957.

IMBELLONI, J. *La Segunda Esfinge Indiana.* Buenos Aires: Librería Hachette, 1956.

JOHNSON, WILLIS FLETCHER. "Pioneers of Mayan Research," *The Outlook*, CXXXIV (July 25, 1923), 474–75.

KENNEDY, JAMES. *Probable Origin of American Indians.* London: E. Lumley, 1854.

McCULLOH, JAMES H. *Researches on America, Being an Attempt To Settle Some Points Relative to the Aborigines of America, &c.* Baltimore: Jos. Robinson, 1817.

MacKINTOSH, JOHN. *The Discovery of America by Christopher Columbus and the Origin of the North American Indians.* Toronto: W. J. Coates, 1836 (The same book appeared later as: JOHN McINTOSH. *The Origin of the North American Indians.* New York: Nafis & Cornish, 1843.)

PAYNE, EDWARD JOHN. *History of the New World Called America.* Oxford: Clarendon Press, 1899.

PRIEST, JOSIAH. *American Antiquities.* Albany: Hoffman & White, 1883.

SHIPP, BARNARD. *The Indian and Antiquities of America.* Philadelphia: Sherman & Co., 1897.

SHORT, JOHN T. *The North Americans of Antiquity.* New York: Harper & Bros., 1880.

STACY-JUDD, ROBERT B. *The Ancient Mayas: Adventures in the Jungles of Yucatan.* Los Angeles: Haskell-Travers, Inc., 1934.

THIERSANT, P. DABRY DE. *De l'Origine des Indiens du Nouveau-Monde et de leur Civilisation.* Paris: Ernest Lerous, 1883.

PHOENICIANS

CABRERA, PABLO FELIX DE. (See Rio below.)

CAFFAREL, PAUL. "Les Phéniciens en Amérique," *I Congrès International des Américanistes*, I, 93–131. Nancy: G. Crépin-Leblond; and Paris: Maisonneuve et Cie, 1875.

JONES, GEORGE. *An Original History of Aboriginal America.* New York: Harper & Bros., 1843.

NEWMAN, JOHN B. *Origin of the Red Man.* New York: John C. Wells, 1852.

RIO, ANTONIO DEL and PAUL FELIX DE CABRERA. *Description of the Ruins of an Ancient City, Discovered near Palenque.* London, 1822.

VASQUEZ, PEDRO. *Memoir of an Eventful Expedition in Central America Resulting in the Discovery of the Idolatrous City of Iximaya...* New York: J. W. Bell, 1850.

EGYPT IN AMERICA

BRASSEUR DE BOURBOURG, CHARLES STEPHEN. *Quatre Lettres sur Le Mexique.* Paris: F. Brachet, 1868.

CAMPBELL, JOHN. "The Traditions of the Ancient Races of Peru and Mexico Identified with Those of the Historical Peoples of the Old World," *I Congrès International des Américanistes,* I, 348–67. Nancy: G. Crépin-Leblond; and Paris: Maisonneuve et Cie, 1875.

COON, CARLETON S. Book review of "I Looked for Adam" by Herbert Wendt, *Man,* March, 1957.

LE PLONGEON, ALICE. *Queen Moo's Talisman: The Fall of the Maya Empire.* New York: Peter Eckler, 1902.

LE PLONGEON, AUGUSTUS L. *Archaeological Communication on Yucatan.* Worcester: C. Hamilton, 1879.

———. *Mayapan and Maya Inscriptions.* Worcester: C. Hamilton, 1881.

———. *Queen Moo and the Egyptian Sphinx.* New York: the author, 1900.

SALISBURY, STEPHEN, JR. *The Mayas, the Sources of Their History. Dr. LePlongeon in Yucatan.* Worcester: Charles Hamilton, 1877.

Smith Alumnae Quarterly, August, 1958, p. 239.

SMITH, G. ELLIOT. *Elephants and Ethnologists.* London: Kegan Paul, Trench, Trubner & Co.; and New York: E. P. Dutton & Co., 1924.

———. *Human History* New York: W. W. Norton & Co., 1929.

VERRILL, A. HYATT. *Old Civilizations of the New World.* Indianapolis: The Bobbs-Merrill Co., 1929.

VERRILL, A. HYATT, and RUTH VERRILL. *America's Ancient Civilizations.* New York: G. P. Putnam's Sons, 1953.

ATLANTIS AND MU

ADAMS, HERBERT B. "Life and Works of Brasseur de Bourbourg," *Proceedings of the American Antiquarian Society,* VII, 274–90. Worcester, 1891.

BLACKET, W. S. *Researches into the Lost Histories of America.* London: Trübner & Co., 1883.

BRASSEUR DE BOURBOURG, CHARLES STEPHEN. (See *Egypt in America* above.)

BUELNA, EUSTAQUIO. *La Atlántida y la Última Tule.* Mexico: Secretaría de Fomento, 1895.

CERVE, W. S. *Lemuria—The Lost Continent of the Pacific.* San Jose, Calif.: Rosicrucian Press, n.d.

CHIL Y NARANJO. "L'Atlantide," *I Congrès International des Américanistes,* I, 163–66. Nancy: G. Crépin-Leblond; and Paris: Maisonneuve et Cie, 1875.

CHURCHWARD, JAMES. *The Cosmic Forces of Mu.* New York: Ives Washburn, Inc., 1934.

———. *The Lost Continent of Mu.* New York: Ives Washburn, Inc., 1932.

DONNELLY, IGNATIUS. *Atlantis: The Antediluvian World.* New York: Harper & Bros., 1880.

HOSKINS, WILLIAM WALTON. *Atlantis and Other Poems.* Philadelphia: Sherman & Co., 1881.

HOWARD, GEORGE. "Seeking the Lost Continent under the Atlantic," *Rosicrucian Digest,* XXVIII (August, 1950), 248–51.

MERRILL, E. D. "Scuttling Atlantis and Mu," *American Scholar,* III (1936), 142–48.

RUDE, GILBERT. "A Survey of Atlantis," *U.S. Naval Institute Proceedings,* Vol. LXVI, No. 8, Whole No. 450 (August, 1940), pp. 1105–23. Annapolis.

SPENCE, LEWIS. *Atlantis in America.* London: Ernest Benn, Ltd., 1925.

———. *The Problem of Atlantis.* Rev. ed. New York: Brentano's, 1925.

WILLARD, R. A. (THEODORE). *The City of the Sacred Well.* London: Willaim Heinemann, Ltd., 1926.

WILSON, SIR DANIEL. *The Lost Atlantis and Other Ethnographic Studies.* New York: Macmillan & Co., 1892.

ISRAELITES IN AMERICA

ADAIR, JAMES. *The History of the American Indians.* London: E. and C. Dilly, 1775.

BERTRAND, L. A. *Mémoires d'un Mormon.* Paris: E. Jung-Treuttel, n.d.

BLUMENTHAL, WALTER HART. *In Old America.* New York: Walton Book Co., 1931.

BOUDINOT, ELIAS. *A Star in the West; or, A Humble Attempt To Discover the Long Lost Ten Tribes of Israel, Preparatory to the Return to their Beloved City, Jerusalem.* Trenton, N.J.: D. Fenton, S. Hutchinson, & J. Dunham, 1816.

DRAKE, SAMUEL G. (See *General* above.)

FERGUSON, THOMAS STUART. *One Fold and One Shepherd.* San Francisco: Books of California, 1958.

GARCÍA, GREGORIO. *Origen de los Indios en el Nuevo Mundo e Indias Occidentales.* Madrid: F. M. Abad, 1729.

GODBEY, ALLEN H. *The Lost Tribes a Myth: Suggestions towards Rewriting Hebrew History.* Durham, N.C.: Duke University Press, 1930.

HILLS, LEWIS EDWARD. *New Light on American Archaeology.* Independence, Mo.: Lambert Moon Printing Co., 1924.

HUNTER, MILTON R. and THOMAS STUART FERGUSON. *Ancient America and the Book of Mormon.* Oakland, Calif.: Kolob Book Co., 1950.

ISRAEL, MENASSEH BEN JOSEPH BEN. *Origen de los Americanos, Esto es Esperanza de Israel.* Madrid: S. Perez Junquera, 1881.

JAKEMAN, M. WELLS. "An Unusual Tree-of-Life Sculpture from Ancient Central America," *Bulletin of the University Archaeological Society,* No. 4 (March, 1953), pp. 26–49. Provo, Utah.

JIJÓN Y CAAMAÑO, JACINTO. "Edward King—Visconde de Kingsborough (1795–1837)," *Boletín de la Sociedad Ecuatoriana de Estudios Históricos Americanos,* Vol. I (June, 1918 [i.e., 1919]).

JONES, EPAPHRAS. *On the Ten Tribes of Israel, and the Aborigines of America, &c. &c.* New Albany, Indiana: Collins & Green, 1831.

KENNEDY, JAMES. (See *General* above.)

KINGSBOROUGH, EDWARD KING, LORD. *Antiquities of Mexico.* 9 vols. London: Robert Havell and Colnaghi, Son, & Co., 1831–48.

MATHER, COTTON. *Magnalia Christi Americana.* 1702.

O'DEA, THOMAS F. *The Mormons.* Chicago: University of Chicago Press, 1957.

RIVERO, MARIANO EDWARD and JOHN JAMES VON TSCHUDI. *Peruvian Antiquities.* New York: George P. Putnam & Co., 1853.

ROO, P. DE. *History of America before Columbus.* 2 vols. Philadelphia and London: J. B. Lippincott Co., 1900.

WOODFORD, IRENE BRIGGS. "The 'Tree of Life' in Ancient America: Its Representation and Significance," *Bulletin of the University Archaeological Society,* No. 4 (March 1953), pp. 1–18. Provo, Utah.

THEOSOPHISTS AND ROSICRUCIANS

ALBERSHEIM, WALTER J. "Science and Mysticism," *Rosicrucian Digest,* XXXI, No. 4 (April, 1953), 140–43, 147–48. San Jose, Calif.

BLAVATSKY, H. P. *The Secret Doctrine.* 1883 edition, Vol. I, pp. 43–44. Quoted in the *Theosophical Quarterly,* XXXII (January, 1935), 196.

GEORG, EUGEN. *The Adventure of Mankind.* New York: E. P. Dutton, 1931.

HEINDEL, MAX. *The Rosicrucian Cosmo-Conception, or Mystic Christianity.* Oceanside, Calif.: The Rosicrucian Fellowship, 1929.

LEADER, HERMAN. "Popol Vuh, a Sacred Book," *Rosicrucian Digest,* XXXII, No. 2 (February, 1954), 69–73. San Jose, Calif.

LEWIS, H. SPENCER. *Rosicrucian Questions and Answers with Complete History of the Rosicrucian Order.* San Jose, Calif.: Rosicrucian Press, 1932.

PREECHE, HAROLD. "Culdee Sages of the Caves," *Rosicrucian Digest,* XXVIII, No. 7 (August, 1950), 259–65. San Jose, Calif.

PREECHE, HAROLD. "When Was America Settled?" *Rosicrucian Digest*, XXXII, No. 2 (February, 1954), 64–68. San Jose, Calif.

WRIGHT, CLAUDE FALLS. *An Outline of the Principles of Modern Theosophy*. Boston and New York, 1894.

FREE-WHEELING LINGUISTICS

DENISEN, T. S. *Mexican Linguistics*. Chicago: T. S. Denisen & Co., 1913.

PARAVEY, M. DE. *Mémoire de M. de Paravey sur l'Origine Japonaise, Arabe, et Basque de la Civilisation des Peoples du Plateau de Bogota*. Paris, 1835.

ROSNY, LUCIEN DE. *Étude de'Archéologie Americain Comparée*. (n.d., no place.)

THIERSANT, DABRY P. DE. (see *General* above.)

WIENER, LEO. *Mayan and Mexican Origins*. Cambridge: Privately Printed, 1926.

WISE, JENNINGS C. *The Red Man in the New World Drama*. Washington, D.C.: W. F. Roberts Co., 1931.

———. *America: The Background of Columbus*. Charlottesville, Va.: Monticello Publishers, 1945.

TRANS-PACIFIC CONTACT

ADAM, LUCIEN. "Du Fou-Sang," *I Congrès International des Américanistes*, I, 144–61. Nancy: G. Crépin-Leblond; and Paris: Maisonneuve et Cie, 1875.

ANONYMOUS. Book review of *Aku-Aku* by Thor Heyerdahl, *Time*, LXXII (September 8, 1958), 100.

ARNOLD, CHANNING, and FREDERICK J. TABOR FROST. *The American Egypt*. New York: Doubleday, Page & Co., 1909.

BENNETT, WENDELL C. Book review of *American Indians in the Pacific* by Thor Heyerdahl, *New York Times*, August 9, 1953, p. 1.

EKHOLM, GORDON F. "A Possible Focus of Asiatic Influence in the Late Classic Cultures of Mesoamerica," *Society for American Archaeology*, Memoir 9, pp. 72–89. Salt Lake City, 1953.

ESTRADA, EMILIO, and BETTY J. MEGGERS. "A Complex of Traits of Probable Transpacific Origin on the Coast of Ecuador," *American Anthropologist*, LXIII, No. 5 (October, 1961), 913–39. Menasha, Wis.

ESTRADA, EMILIO, BETTY J. MEGGERS, and CLIFFORD EVANS. "Possible Transpacific Contact on the Coast of Ecuador," *Science*, CXXXV, No. 3501 (February 2, 1962), 371–72.

GLADWIN, HAROLD STERLING. *Men Out of Asia*. New York: McGraw-Hill Book Co., Inc., 1947.

HEINE-GELDERN, ROBERT, and GORDON F. EKHOLM. "Significant Parallels in the Symbolic Arts of Southern Asia and Middle America," in SOL TAX (ed.), *The Civilizations of Ancient America*, pp. 299–309. Chicago: University of Chicago Press, 1951.

HEYERDAHL, THOR. *Kon-Tiki*. Chicago: Rand McNally & Co., 1950.

————. *American Indians in the Pacific: The Theory behind the Kon-Tiki Expedition*. London, Oslo, and Stockholm: George Allen & Unwin, 1952.

————. *Aku-Aku: The Secret of Easter Island*. Chicago: Rand McNally & Co., 1958.

KROEBER, ALFRED L. *Anthropology*. New York: Harcourt, Brace & Cc., 1948.

KROGMAN, W. M. Book review of *American Indians in the Pacific* by Thor Heyerdahl, *Chicago Sunday Tribune*, July 26, 1953, p. 6.

LINTON, RALPH. Book review of *Men Out of Asia* by Harold S. Gladwin, *American Antiquity*, XIII, No. 4, Pt. 1, 331–32. Menasha, Wis.

————. Book review of *American Indians in the Pacific* by Thor Heyerdahl, *American Anthropologist*, LVI (February, 1954), 122–24. Menasha, Wis.

LOTHROP, SAMUEL K. "Random Thoughts on *Men Out of Asia*," *American Anthropologist*, L, No. 3, Pt. 1, 568–71. Menasha, Wis.

NICOLSON, NIGEL. Book review of *Aku-Aku* by Thor Heyerdahl, *New Statesman*, LV (April 15, 1958), 442.

NORBECK, EDWARD. Book review of *American Indians of the Pacific* by Thor Heyerdahl, *American Antiquity*, XIX, No. 1, 92–94. Salt Lake City.

MACKINTOSH, J. (See *General* above.)

PLISCHKE, HANS. "The Colonization of Polynesia—A Reply to Thor Heyerdahl," *Universitas*, I, No. 4, 397–404. Nancy: G. Crépin-Leblond; and Paris: Maisonneuve et Cie, 1875.

SPOEHR, ALEXANDER. "A Close Look at *Kon-Tiki*," *Chicago Natural History Museum Bulletin*, XXII (July, 1951), 6.

BERING STRAIT

BYERS, DOUGLAS S. "The Bering Bridge—Some Speculations," *Ethnos*, Nos. 1–2, pp. 20–26. Stockholm, 1957.

CARTER, GEORGE F. *Pleistocene Man at San Diego*. Baltimore: Johns Hopkins Press, 1957.

FLINT, RICHARD FOSTER. *Glacial and Pleistocene Geology*. New York: John Wiley & Sons, Inc. 1957.

GRIFFIN, JAMES B. "Some Prehistoric Connections between Siberia and America," *Science*, CXXXI, No. 3403 (March 18, 1960). Washington, D.C.

INDEX

Aac: king of Uxmal, 12–13
Abyssinians, 54
Acapulco, 15
Acosta, Joseph de, 31
Adair, James, 5, 57
Adam, Lucien, 92, 101
Adam and Eve, 12; *see also* Garden of Eden
Afghans, 54
Africans, 3, 74; *see also* Akka; Egypt; Mandingoes; Zulus
Agassiz, Louis, 117
Agriculture, 87–88
Akka, 105
Aku Aku; see Heyerdahl, Thor
Alaska, 21 n.; *see also* Bering Strait
Albersheim, Walter J., 80
Alexander the Great, 2; *see also* Gladwin, Harold S.
Alphabet, 32

American Antiquarian Society, 19
Andes; *see* Inca; Peru
Anglo-Saxons, 54
Antilia, 30, 31
Ark, 55, 63
Arnold, Channing, and Frederick J. Tabor Frost, 26, 90–91, 93, 95, 96
Asia, 4, 69, 93–96, 96–97
Assyrians, 3, 18
Athenians, 30
Atlantean figures, 26
Atlantis: appeals to mystics, 28; a continuing theory, 4, 27; Heindel's description of, 43–44; history of the theory, 30–32; home of mystics' fourth root-race, 123; Lost Continent of, 28–49; Queen Moo flees to, 12; theory compared to Bering Strait hypothesis, 85–86

Atlas, 32–33, 62
Avalon, 30
Aztecs, 3, 5

BACON, Francis, 32
Baker, De Vere, 107–8
Balboa, Vasco Núñez de, 1
Baldwin, John D., 56, 117
Bananas, 105
Bancroft, Hubert Howe: on Brasseur de Bourbourg, 48–49, 126; on Brooks' Peru-China theory, 107; critique of Ranking's Kublai Khan theory, 89; on Lord Kingsborough, 52–53
Basques, 3, 110
Belshazzar, 20
Bennett, Wendell C., 76–77, 107
Bering Strait, 4, 51, 83–84, 85, 86
Bertrand, L. A., 61
Bird, Junius, 76
Blacket, W. S., 33
Blavatsky, H. P.: criticized scientists, 80–81; esoteric writing of, 130; mystic cosmology of, 42; said Theosophy teaches esoteric history, 131; views on evolution and race, 122–24
Book of Mormon, The: Articles of Faith for, 59; compared with Annals of Ixtlilxochitl, 62, 63; describes Israelite wanderings in America, 4, 5; not concerned with Lost Tribes, 59; sailing craft described in, 59; see also Mormons
Borbolla, Daniel Rubin de la, 76
Brasseur de Bourbourg, Charles Stephen, 44–49; Bancroft's critique of, 126; compared with G. Elliot Smith, 21; Egyptian theory of, 25; Le Plongeon did not want name linked with, 20–

21; lost professional reputation, 5; in Rome
Brazil, 44
Breadfruit, 105
Brigham Young University, 64–65
Bronze, 88
Brooks, Charles Wolcott, 107
Bryan, William Jennings, 2
Buddhists: Buddhism related to American religions, 92; identified with American Indians, 3; paper on, at Nancy, 99; route to America, 95; voyage from Ceylon to Java, 95
Buffon, Georges Louis Leclerc de, 31
Burmese, 54
Byers, Douglas S., 86

CABRERA, Pablo Felix de, 128
Caicédo, Torrès, 100
Cambodia, 24, 65
Canaanites, 3, 55, 57
Canary Islands, 21 n., 33, 98
Carter, George F., 84 n.
Carthaginians; see Phoenicians
Cataclysms, 35
Catherwood, Frederick, 14; 15
Cay, Prince of Yucatan, 12–13
Cenote of Sacrifice, Chichen Itza, Yucatan; see Sacred Cenote
Cereals, 87
Chac Mool, 8–9, 11, 16–17
Charlevoix, Pierre de, 85
Chichen Itza, Yucatan, Mexico: Asiatic influences at, 93; Atlantean figures at, 26; bearded figures in sculpture, 9, 18; Chac Mool discovered there, 17; king of, 11; Le Plongeon in, 8; Sacred Cenote of, 33
Chil y Narango, Dr., 29, 98
Chinese: colonized America, 74;

dolmens, 24; Fo related to American religions, 92; identified with American Indians, 3; relationships with Peru, 107; relics in Peru, 92; route of Lost Tribes of Israel, 51

Church of Jesus Christ of Latter-day Saints; see Mormons

Churchward, James, 36; religious leanings, 117–18; on tablets of Mu, 39–40; writing style of, 129

Churchward, William, 37–38

Circumcision, 55

Coh, Prince of Yucatan, 12–13, 16

Coconuts, 87, 105

Cogolludo, Diego Lopez de, 109

Colombia, 110

Columbus, Christopher, 1; looked for Antilia, 30

Confession among American Indians, 55

Copan ruins, Honduras, 25

Corbeled arch, 88

Cortez, Hernán, 10

Cotton, 87

Cozumel Island, Yucatan, Mexico; 17, 108

Critias of Plato, 29–30

Cro-Magnon race, 119–20

Crops; see Agriculture

Cumorah, Hill of, 61

DALL, W. H., 134–35

D'Aristarchi, Stéphane, 98

Darrow, Clarence, 2

Del Río, Antonio, 45–46

Denisen, T. S., 71, 81

Diving gods, in Asia and America, 93–94

Dixon, Roland B., 22–25; 64

D'Oliver, Fabre, 44

Domesticated animals, 87–88

Donnelly, Ignatius: on Atlantis, 4; on cataclysms, 35; map of Atlantis, 34; urged search for Atlantis, 36 n.

Drake, Samuel G., 81

Dravidian; see India

Duran, Father, 53 n.

EARTHQUAKES, 16

Easter Island, 2, 62

Ecuador, 96–97

Eden, Garden of; see Garden of Eden

Egypt: colonized from Atlantis, 48; cradle of civilization, 3; influence in ancient America, 7–27 *passim*; settled by colonizers from Mu, 39; sun worship derived from Atlantis, 32

Egyptian inscriptions, 27

Egyptians, 3

Ekholm, Gordon F., and Robert Heine-Geldern, 93–94

Elephants depicted on Maya sculpture, 25

Eliot, John, favored Lost Tribes theory, 53 n.

Elysian Fields, 32

Estrada, Emilio, Betty J. Meggers, and Clifford Evans, 96–97

Etruscans, 3

Evans, Clifford; see Estrada, Emilio, Betty J. Meggers, and Clifford Evans

Eve; see Adam and Eve

Evolution, 2, 122–24

FERGUSON, Thomas Stuart, 62, 66, 74

Fez, Morocco, 35

Field, Stephen J., 15

Finno-Ugrian, 108

Flint, Richard Foster, 83

Flood myths: among American Indians, 55; in *Annals of Ixtlilxochitl*, 63; Dixon's study of, 64; in native Indian books, 64

Food; *see* Agriculture

Fortunate Islands, 30

Foster, John W., 17

Fracastoro, Giralamo, 31 n.

French, 3

Frost, Frederick J. Tabor; *see* Arnold, Channing, and Frederick J. Tabor Frost

Fruit trees; *see* Agriculture

Fu-Sang theory: attacked by de Hellwald, 101–2; Chinese reached America, 90; defined, 29; reviewed by Adam, 101

GAFFAREL, Paul, 98

Gambling, 88

García, Gregorio, 53 n., 109, 120–2

García, Rejón, 109

Garden of Eden, 12, 32; *see also* Adam and Eve

Gardens of the Hesperides, 32

Gardner, Martin, 125

Genesis, author of, 12

Georg, Eugen, 130

Gerland, George, 106

Gladwin, Harold S.: Alexander's Fleet theory, 89; asked Hooton to write preface, 82; attacked professional anthropologists, 71–72, 75–76; on cultural retrogression, 41; reviewed by Linton, 2

Godbey, Allen H., 53 n., 56–57

Gourd, 87, 104, 105

Greece: colonized America, 3, 74; deities identified with Atlantean gods, 32; elements of mythology in Tree of Life sculptures, 65; flotilla in Yucatan waters, 112; linguistic affiliations with Maya, 18; Macedonian arms found in Brazil, 44

Griffin, James B., 84 n.

HAECKEL, Ernst; *see* Jaekel, Ernst

Hebrews; *see* Israelites

Heindel, Max, 42, 121–22, 122–24

Heine-Geldern, Robert; *see* Ekholm, Gordon F. and Robert Heine-Geldern

Hellwald, Frédéric de, 100–101, 102

Herodotus, 18

Hesperides; *see* Gardens of the Hesperides

Heyerdahl, Thor: and attraction to mystics, 5, 132–33; on cultural retrogression, 41; and large popular following, 4; opposed in New York, 70; presentation of theory, 127–28; theories accepted on slim evidence, 112–13; theory regarding Peruvian population of Polynesia, 103–7; views on race, 120; voyage to support theory, 5

Hieroglyphic writing, 7, 11, 79

Hills, Lewis Edward, method used by, 131–32; revelation to, 68; writings of, 67

Hindus: astrology compared with Mexican, 91; deities compared with Mexican gods, 91; deities identified with Atlantean gods, 32; identified with American Indians, 3; Theosophists' orientation toward, 118–19

Hooton, Earnest Albert, 33, 77, 82

Horses, 25–26

Horus, Egyptian god, 48

House types, 96

Huipil, Maya women's tunic, 18

Humboldt, Alexander von, 36, 91
Huns, 3
Hunter, Milton R., 61–62, 74
Hwui Shan and the Fu-Sang fable, 91

IMBELLONI, J., 31 n.
Inca, 3, 5
India: Dravidian temples, 24; mummification in, 21; settled by colonizers from Mu, 39; Sammono-Cadom related to American religions, 92
International Congress of Americanists, 97–102
Intoxicants, 88
Irish, 3
Iron, 88
Isis, 13
Isle of Seven Cities, 30
Israelites: identified with American Indians, 3; Lost Tribes hypothesis favored by early writers, 3; Lost Tribes theory, 50–58; Mormons deny Lost Tribes in their doctrine, 59; Mormon doctrine on, 59–68; theory perseveres, 27; voyage from Red Sea to Central America, 108; see also Mormons
Ixtlilxochitl, Fernando de Alva, 62

JAEKEL, Ernst, 38
Japan: Buddhism related to American religions, 92; ceramic resemblances in Ecuador, 96; Japanese descended from Lost Tribes of Israel, 54; linguistic affiliation with Muysca of Colombia, 110
Jaredites, 58–59
Java, 65
Jefferson, Thomas, 4

Jesus, 19, 20, 61
Jijón e Caamaño, Jacinto, 52
Johnson, Willis Fletcher, 78–80
Jones, Epaphras, 117, 119, 132
Jones, George, 116
Josselyn, John, 85

KAFFIRS, 54
Karens, 54
Kennedy, James, 56, 117
Khmers, 96
Kingsborough, Edward King, Viscount, 5, 51–52
Klaproth, H. J. von, 91
Kon-Tiki; see Heyerdahl, Thor
Koreans, 90
Kroeber, Alfred L., 113
Krogman, W. M., 106–7
Kublai Khan, 89
Kwakiutl Indians, 103

LAMAISM, 92
Lamanites, 59–60
Landa, Bishop Diego de, 57
Language: amateur research in, 108–13; attraction for mystics, 6; Polynesian distribution, 105; supports theory of migrations from Polynesia into Pacific, 106
Las Casas, Bartolomé de, 53 n.
Lehi, 59, 107
Lemuria; see Mu
Lemurian Fellowship, 118
Le Plongeon, Alice: her death-bed revelations, 19–20; her friend's interest in Atlantis, 133–34; her necrology of her husband, 15, 16, 20
Le Plongeon, Augustus, 7–21; bitter over lack of recognition, 78–79; on Chinese relics in Peru, 92; criticized professional anthropologists, 73; Egyptian the-

ory of, 25; his anti-Christian leanings, 117; his theories rejected, 5; on Maya language affiliations, 108; and travels, 15
L'Estrange, Sir Hamon, 55
Lewis, H. Spencer, 31, 133
Lewis, Ralph M., 70
Linguistics; see Language
Linton, Ralph, 2, 107
Lisbon, Portugal, 35
Li Yen, 90–91
López de Gómara, Francisco, 31 n., 53 n.
Lost Continent of Atlantis; see Atlantis
Lost Continent of Mu; see Mu
Lost Tribes of Israel; see Israelites
Lothrop, Samuel Kirkland, 41–42, 89–90
Lotus motif, 93–94

MACAWS: Maya stylizations resemble elephants, 24, 25
McCulloh, James H., 41
Macedonia; see Greece
MacKintosh, John: attacked Lost Tribes theory, 56; favored Korean theory, 90; on origin of name Yucatan, 109; warned against trusting linguistic similarities, 111
Madagascans, 3
Magellan, Fernando, 1
Magoun, H. W., 119
Malays, 54, 106
Mandingoes, 3
Mango-Capac, 92
Marriage restrictions, 55
Masai, 54
Masonry, Free, 11
Mather, Cotton, 53 n., 85, 115
Mather, Increase, 53 n.
Maudslay, Alfred Percival, 26

Maury, Matthew Fontaine, 92
Maya: Carthaginian-Phoenician traits among, 3; gods compared with Hindu, 91; Le Plongeon's study of, 5; linguistic affiliations with Sanskrit, 111; pyramids, 24; vigesimal system, 90; See also Chichen Itza, Yucatan; Copan, Honduras; Hieroglyphic writing; Huipil; Sacred Cenote; Uxmal
Meggers, Betty J.; see Estrada, Emilio, Betty J. Meggers, and Clifford Evans
Mennasseh ben Israel, ben Joseph, 53, 116
Merrill, E. D., 135
Metallurgy, 32; see also Iron; Bronze
Mexico: Brasseur de Bourbourg in, 46–47; crossed by Le Plongeon, 15; pyramids of, 24; see also Acapulco; Aztecs; Chichen Itza; Cozumel Island; Maya; Oaxaca; Toltecs; Tula; Uxmal; Yucatan
Mitchell, J. Leslie, 25
Mohawks, 85
Montaigne, Michel Eyquem de, 31
Moo, Queen of Chichen Itza, 12–13
Mormons (Church of Jesus Christ of Latter-day Saints): and American Indian origins, 3; beliefs described by Bertrand, 61; doctrine on Hebrews in America, 4, 117; racist views of, 121; see also Book of Mormon, The; Brigham Young University; Baker, De Vere; Ferguson, Thomas Stuart; Hills, Louis Edward; Hunter, Milton R.; Lehi; Lamanites; Nephites; Tree of Life
Morse, E., 91

Morse, Samuel F. B., 19
Morton, Thomas, 85, 111
Moses, 39, 64
Mu, Lost Continent of, 36–43; atmosphere of, 44; Heindel's description of, 42–43; see also Churchward, James; Churchward, William; Naacal tablets of Mu; Niven, William
Mummification: in Mexico and on Atlantis, 32; in Peru and Egypt, 7; spread from Egypt, 21 n., 23

NAACAL tablets of Mu, 39, 42
Nearchus, 89
Neck rests, 96
Nemo, Captain, 36
Nephites, 59–60
Neuman, Friederich de, 91
New World Archaeological Foundation, 66
Nicte, sister of Queen Moo, 12
Niven, William, 39
Norbeck, Edward, 41, 106, 120, 127–28
Norsemen, 3

OATHS, 88
Oaxaca, Mexico, 27
Ordeals, 88
Oviedo y Valdés, Gonzalo Fernández de, 30, 53 n.
Ox, 87

PACIFIC; see Trans-Pacific contacts; Heyerdahl, Thor; Estrada, Emilio, Betty J. Meggers, and Clifford Evans; Ekholm, Gordon F., and Robert Heine-Geldern
Pagodas, 91
Pan pipes, 88, 96
Parcheesi game, 88

Patolli game, 88
Payne, Edward John, 53 n., 111
Peabody Foundation, Robert S., 86
Peabody Museum of Harvard University, 22
Penn, William, 53 n.
Perry, William J., 21 n.
Persia, 51
Peru: and art similarities with Polynesia, 103; Chinese relics in, 92; decimal system, 90; gods compared with Hindu, 91; Israelites in, 59; Le Plongeon in, 15; linguistic affiliations with Sanskrit, 111; llamas and alpacas in, 88; and Lost Tribes theory, 56; Mochica period, 41; mummification in, 21 n.; relationships with China, 107; see also Inca; Mango-Capac; Heyerdahl, Thor
Petitot, Reverend Father, 100
Phallic cults, 93
Phoenicians, 3, 32, 128
Phuddy Duddy, Dr., 72–73
Pigs, 26
Plato: on Atlantis, 29–30; called "inventor of the noble lie," 134; Critias, 29–30; Timaeus, 29; earliest authority on Atlantis, 3; palace described by, 33
Plischke, Hans, 106
Plow, 87, 91
Polynesia, 4; see also Breadfruit; Coconuts; Heyerdahl, Thor; Language
Popol Vuh, 63
Portuguese, 3
Prescott, William H., 46
Priest, Josiah, 55
Pyramids: Brasseur's theory on, 47–48; Egyptian theory exploded, 24–25; Maya compared

with pagodas, 91; spread from Egypt, 21

QUETZALCOATL: identified with Horus, 48; identified with Jesus, 61; identified with many characters, 62; a missionary of Brahma or Buddha worship, 92; reincarnated in Cortez, 10

RACE, 32, 42
Racism, 119–24
Ranking, John, 88–89
Rejón García, Manuel, 25–26
Religion; see Theology
Richmond Brown, Lady, 41
Río, Antonio del; see Del Río, Antonio
Rivero, Mariano Edward, 56, 92
Roman inscriptions, 27
Romans: flotilla in Yucatan waters, 112; fort at Marietta on Ohio River, 55; identified with American Indians, 3
Rosicrucians: accused professional scientists, 80; beliefs about Atlantis, 31; interested in American Indian origins, 3; interested in Atlantis and Mu, 4; methods used by, 133; and religious interests, 118; writing style of, 131; see also Heindel, Max
Rosny, Léon de, 99–100, 101
Rosny, Lucien de, 63, 110
Rude, Gilbert, 129
Ruysch's map of 1508, 30

SACRED Cenote, Chichen Itza, Yucatan, 33
Sacrifices: among American Indians, 55; on Canary Islands, 33;

at Chichen Itza, Yucatan, 33; Morning Star ceremony, 62
St. Brendan's Isle, 30
Sanskrit, 18
Scandinavians, 32
Scotland, 119–20
Sculpture, Maya, 9, 18
Scythians, 3, 85
Sewall, Samuel, 53 n.
Short, John T., 13–14
Sinnett, A. P., 42, 122–24
Smith, G. Elliot, 21–25 passim
Smith, Joseph, 61
Solomon, King, 25
Sommono-Cadom, 92
Spaniards, 3
Spence, Lewis: did not want name linked with Brasseur or Le Plongeon, 21; on durability of Atlantis theory, 131; equated Quetzalcoatl with Atlas, 32; foresaw disapproval, 81; racist views of, 119–20; on scientific and mystic method, 131; writer on Atlantis, 4, 31
Spencer, Herbert, 125
Spinden, Herbert J., 77
Spoehr, Alexander, 104–5
Stacy-Judd, Robert B., 132, 133
Stanley, Henry Morton, 105
Stephens, John Lloyd, 14, 15
Stonehenge, 2
Sunday, Billy, 67
Sun worship, 7
Sweet potato, 87, 104, 105

TARO, 105
Tartars, 3, 85
Tepexpan Man, Mexico, 40
Theology, 6, 115–19
Theosophists: beliefs about Atlantis, 31–32; religious interests, 118–19; interested in

American Indian origins, 3; interested in Atlantis and Mu, 4

Thiersant, P. Dabry de, 111; *see also* Blavatsky, H. P.; Georg, Eugen

Thrones, 93

Tibet, 92

Tie-dyeing, 88

Tile, 91

Timaeus of Plato, 29

Toltecs, 31, 47, 123

Torquemada, Tomás de, 53 n.

Toscanelli's chart, 30

Tozzer, Alfred Marston, 22, 25

Trans-Pacific contacts: evidence for and against, 88–102; growing support for, 5; *see also* Ekholm, Gordon F., and Robert Heine-Geldern; Estrada, Emilio, Betty J. Meggers, and Clifford Evans; Arnold, Channing, and Frederick J. Tabor Frost

Tree of Life, 64–65

Troana Codex, 48

Tschudi, John James von: opposed Lost Tribes theory, 56; saw common origin of Far Eastern and American religions, 92

Tula, Mexico, 93

Tulane University, 33, 59, 110–111

Turkeys, 88

Turkish, 85

Tyrians; *see* Phoenicians

Utatlan, Guatemala, 33; 110–11

Uxmal, Yucatan, 12

Veracruz, Mexico, 15, 46

Verne, Jules, 36

Verrill, Mr. and Mrs. A. Hyatt: accused professional anthropologists, 74; claimed approval of professional anthropologists, 76, 82; foresaw disapproval, 81

Viollet-le-Duc, 91

Voltaire, 31, 117

Waldeck, Jean Frederick, 109

Well, Sacred; *see* Sacred Cenote, Chichen Itza, Yucatan

Welsh, 3

Wheel: Gladwin's accusations, 75–76; not in New World, 87, 91; Verrill's accusations, 74–77 *passim*

Wiener, Leo, 77, 111

Willard, Theodore A., 57

Williams, Roger, 53 n.

Winthrop, Robert C., 98

Wise, Jennings C.: linguistic theories, 111–12; on d'Olivet's Mu, 44; on origin of name Lemuria, 38–39; religious leanings, 118; thought shape of continents symbolic, 134

Wood, William, 55

Wright, Claude Falls, 122–24; 44

Yellow fever, 16

Yémon, Ogivia, 98

Yucatan, Mexico: Egyptian-like sculptures in, 26; origin of name, 109–10

Zarito, Agustin de: championed Atlantis theory, 31 n. 2

Zélinski, Luis de, 98

Zero, 88

Zodiac signs: Hindu compared with Mexican, 91

Zulus: descended from Lost Tribes of Israel, 54